CASE STUDIES FROM THE
WESTERN CLASSICAL REPERTORY

Kay Kaufman Shelemay

W·W·NORTON & COMPANY · NEW YORK · LONDON

Copyright © 2001 by W. W. Norton & Company, Inc.

All rights reserved
Printed in the United States of America
First Edition

Library of Congress Cataloging-in-Publication Data

Shelemay, Kay Kaufman.
  Soundscapes classical: case studies from the Western classical repertory/Kay Kaufman Shelemay.
    p. cm.
  ISBN 0-393-97703-X (pbk.)
    1. Music appreciation. 2. Music—History and criticism. I. Shelemay, Kay Kaufman.
Soundscapes.
  MT90 .S53 2001 Suppl.
780′.9—dc21   00-067566

W. W. Norton & Company, Inc., 500 Fifth Avenue, New York, N.Y. 10110
www.wwnorton.com
W. W. Norton & Company Ltd., Castle House, 75/76 Wells Street, London W1T 3QT
1 2 3 4 5 6 7 8 9 0

Contents

Preface

The musical vocabulary of the Western tonal tradition has had a pervasive influence on musical styles around the world. This influence, as we will see throughout *Soundscapes,* began long before immigrants brought their music to North America. The system of Western tonal music spread beyond European shores in various ways: by a colonial presence in places as distant as Vietnam, Hawaii, and South Africa; by performances of touring European and American musicians abroad; and by sound recordings, radio, movies, and television (See **"Studying Music: Thinking about Western Music"** in chapter 2).

The repertory initially responsible for spreading the Western musical language was the liturgy of the Christian church. The early presence of Western Christian missions in far-flung areas of Africa, Asia, and the Middle East introduced and transmitted the sound of Western sacred music internationally. Later, especially with the establishment of Western colonial governments in the nineteenth century, the secular repertories of military bands and performances of "Western classical music" also gained significant influence. The expression "Western classical music" in widespread use generally refers to art music produced by European and North American composers in the eighteenth through twentieth centuries. It is this large repertory of notated instrumental and vocal works that stands at the center of the tonal musical style, a style that is also shared by a wide range of European musics transmitted in the oral tradition. Whether spread indirectly through hymns or the increasingly ubiquitous piano, the language of Western classical music penetrated cultural boundaries. Western music has also absorbed musical influences, bringing back to Europe, and later to North America, echoes of other styles such as the Turkish Janissary band, which influenced Haydn, Mozart, and Beethoven, and the Indonesian gamelan, which left its traces in music of Debussy.

European colonizers in the New World brought with them the Western classical musical tradition, along with many performers and educational practices. This tradition quickly assumed a position of cultural dominance with the economic and political elite of North America. In the nineteenth century, American cities saw the founding of music conservatories, planting the seeds for the present-day teaching of European music history from the Middle Ages to the present in most American colleges and universities. Americans welcomed the establishment of symphony orchestras and opera houses in major cities. They began to participate actively in amateur musical activities, such as taking piano lessons at home and singing in community choral societies. This wide and deep stream of Western classical music and music education has continued to be important in American musical life. Not surprisingly, as immigrants brought many other musical traditions to America, new styles including a range of African American repertories gained widespread and enthusiastic followings, and the Western classical tradition began to interact with and respond to the musical diversity around it.

This booklet explores two Western classical works for each chapter of *Soundscapes*. We will generally examine the setting from which a piece emerged, including the time and place of its composition and the work's position within the creative output of its composer. Only after we have looked at the setting and intended significance of the piece and its relationship to the chapter topic will we turn to the sound, expanding *Soundscapes'* musical vocabulary with terms commonly used in connection with Western music. In some cases, we will also address how a work's settings, sounds, and significances, as well as our perception of them, have changed over time.

A Note to
the Instructor

Soundscapes Classical supplements chapters 1–10 of *Soundscapes* by discussing the
settings, sounds, and significances of selected works from the Western classical-
music repertory. In this way, compositions ranging from the madrigal to musical
comedy are approached within the same framework as other musical traditions in
the book, providing an opportunity for contrast and comparison. To insure easy
accessibility, all of the compositions discussed here are contained on the 8-CD set,
The Norton Recordings to Accompany the Enjoyment of Music, and most may be
found on the 4-CD-ROM set, *The Norton Recordings, Shorter Version.* For each
chapter, two works provide classical perspectives on important issues; instructors
should feel free—indeed encouraged—to supplement or replace these with other
compositions of their own choice. Beginning with chapter 5, we will follow a rough
historical continuum to incorporate musics of different eras and styles that speak
to the main topic of each chapter in *Soundscapes.* Our historical survey begins with
two works composed before 1600 that illustrate the subject of worship and belief.
The discussion in chapter 6 of music and dance incorporates two eighteenth-
century compositions that had their genesis in the dance. For chapter 7, which
explores music and memory, we investigate a composition from the eighteenth century and another from the early nineteenth that demonstrate Western classical
music's interaction with and impact on memory, while the mid-nineteenth century
provides two works that exemplify the topic of chapter 8, how music expresses

identity. The subject of chapter 9, music and politics, arises in two strikingly different compositions from the first half of the twentieth century, and our final topic, music in the real world, covered in chapter 10, is illustrated by two works that stretch the boundaries of the classical canon in the mid-twentieth century.

This booklet allows classical-music specialists to teach *Soundscapes* using familiar repertory. At the same time, the instructor should be aware that the textbook itself already incorporates a number of musics that are related in their histories or content to the Western classical repertory and its musical language. Throughout, we encounter compelling evidence of interaction between the Western musical system and the musical systems of other cultures.

The following quick review lists some of these close connections. In chapter 1, we encounter a song about migration still sung by present-day northern Italians, echoing a late-nineteenth-century musical style. Our studies of the bagpipes, lullabies, and the *quinceañera* in chapter 2 span musics with different histories that were shaped in part by European musical influence. In chapter 3, we find Vietnamese musical styles that have interacted with Western popular and classical musics prior to the immigration of Vietnamese people to the United States. We find as well Middle Eastern songs that borrow and elaborate on selected Western classical compositions. The cityscapes of Boston, Houston, and Juneau surveyed in chapter 4 include discussion of orchestras, conservatories, and related ensembles in each of these locales. We can also trace a great deal of musical activity in chapter 4 that crosses domains as different as, say, folk music and early music, all of which have many roots in Euro-American music history. Our studies of several musics of belief in chapter 5 explore how individuals express different belief systems in different musical styles and contexts, and demonstrate as well the cross-cultural importance of chant. The exploration of the dance in chapter 6 features the polka and tango, both of which emerged within Europe or were influenced by European immigrants abroad. We also encounter a South Asian dance style, bhangra, deeply influenced and transformed by aspects of late-twentieth-century British and American popular music and technoculture. In chapter 7, the discussion of music and memory introduces Syrian, Mexican, and African American musical repertories that all support memory, at least in part, through their reliance on familiar Western melodies. Aspects of identity detailed in chapter 8—as expressed by *enka* music for karaoke, by a Persian composer fashioning a concerto, and through contrasting musical styles celebrated by Cajun and Creole populations in Louisiana—each provide sounds that are distinctive but that also draw on aspects of the Euro-American musical language. In chapter 9, too, examples of music as an expression of implicit or open resistance against European or American political and economic control—whether derived from Native American, Caribbean, or South African cultures—demonstrate the domestication and transformation of the very musical traditions that are being disputed. Finally, in chapter 10, we see diverse streams of musical experience flow together to give rise to new combinations, whether a fusion of Mongolian and Tibetan vocal styles with chant or a composition for saxophone and gamelan. Throughout *Soundscapes,* then, you will find that classical-music styles can appear in various transformations, as ingredients in both old and new worlds of hybrid musics. Classical music, too, continues to provide a bridge through which cross-cultural musical instruments, concepts, and sounds reach into the heart of the Euro-American concert hall.

At home today in North America, the multifaceted world of Western classical music is a living tradition. One can easily hear a symphony orchestra, go to a choir concert, play in a string quartet, attend the opera, or learn to play piano or guitar, supporting the thesis that Western classical music can profitably be studied—and should be studied—through the same ethnographic techniques as any other musical tradition.

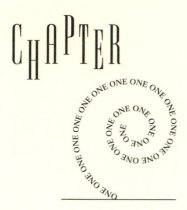

CHAPTER

ONE ONE ONE ONE ONE ONE ONE ONE ONE ONE ONE ONE ONE ONE ONE ONE ONE ONE ONE ONE ONE ONE ONE ONE ONE ONE ONE ONE

Introduction

In chapter 1 of *Soundscapes,* we establish a framework for understanding music and for critical listening. A *soundscape* is a musical culture that is unified in its setting, sound, and significance. For each work, then, first we investigate the *settings* within which a soundscape is performed and the historical paths through which it has traveled to become part of the lives of a particular group. Second, we learn to hear and describe musical *sound,* breaking it into acoustical characteristics of *quality, pitch, duration,* and *intensity* while we also look at indigenous musical concepts. Third, we explore the *significance* of the soundscape, both in its time and place of composition and, if it has changed, at the point where we encounter it. These are the same factors we apply to Tuvan throat singing and to the many other musical traditions we explore throughout *Soundscapes* and this booklet. All of the traditions we study have crossed boundaries of historical time and cultural space and have acquired new meanings. In the case of the Western classical tradition, a diverse array of soundscapes that began in different periods and places in Europe have joined to constitute a "supersoundscape" in North America that has many independent but closely related interacting parts. (We can also refer to the semi-independent yet interrelated nature of Western classical soundscapes as "soundscape clusters," an expression explored at greater length in chapter 4 of *Soundscapes.*) Whenever we refer to Western classical soundscapes, we need to be conscious that a large and flexible umbrella today shelters coexisting musics that originated in very different times and places.

1

CASE STUDY:

The Young Person's Guide to the Orchestra

The Young Person's Guide to the Orchestra, by the twentieth-century British composer Benjamin Britten (1913–1976), is an especially appropriate point of departure for chapter 1 because Britten composed it for the express purpose of introducing the sounds of the instruments in the Western classical orchestra. As in the case of most compositions, information about the genesis of *The Young Person's Guide* and the setting for which it was originally intended can inform our understanding of its sound and its significance. We will start with a brief review of the composer's experiences during World War II.

After a long stay in the United States, Britten returned in March 1942 to his native England, where he spent the remainder of the war years. In 1945, just after World War II ended, Britten was commissioned (that is, he received a paid contract) to compose two works to commemorate the two hundred fiftieth anniversary of the death of the great English composer, Henry Purcell (1659–1695). Britten had studied and performed works of Purcell for years and had credited Purcell's setting of English texts as a model for his own operas. So well known was Britten's love for the music of Purcell that a critic once wrote that the two composers seemed to be "an intricate and unified whole." In the aftermath of the war, Britten's affinity for Purcell must also have signaled a certain degree of pride in his English musical heritage.

In 1946, Britten was commissioned yet again, this time to compose a film score for use by the Ministry of Education to introduce schoolchildren to the instruments of the orchestra. Having just completed two works honoring Purcell, Britten chose to base this next one on a *melody* (a series of pitches arranged in a distinctive shape) borrowed from Purcell. The main melody of *The Young Person's Guide*—which is subtitled *Variations and Fugue on a Theme of Henry Purcell*—is a *hornpipe,* an English sailors' dance originally composed by Purcell for a performance of a play, *Abdelazar, or, The Moor's Revenge.*

The Young Person's Guide contains three large sections, let's call them A, B, and C. Looking at each section in order will help explain the subtitle. (See also "Sound Sources: The Western Orchestra" in chapter 8 of Soundscapes.)

The **A** section of this work contains six statements of the *theme*—the main melody—four of which are changed or varied in some way and are therefore called *variations.* The first unit of this *theme and variations* form, the *statement* of the theme, begins with the entire orchestra playing. After a brief transition, we hear a series of four variations, each performed by a different section of the orchestra.

In the first variation, played by the *woodwind* family, the main theme can be heard very easily. The second variation presents the theme played by the *brass* section. The third variation features the *stringed* instruments, moving from the highest to the lowest members of the string family: the first and second violins, followed by the violas, the cellos, and the double-basses.

In the fourth variation, Britten gives the theme to the percussion instruments, most of which have no fixed pitch. The timpani, among the few Western percussion instruments that can be tuned, sounds the first three notes of the theme, and then the cymbal, snare drum, tambourine, and triangle all join in, creating a somewhat unconventional melody with their different qualities of sound.

The four variations are followed by a return to the melody as it was originally presented by the entire orchestra at the beginning of section **A.**

Section **B** also consists of variations on Purcell's theme and it, too, is organized by instrumental families, beginning with the woodwinds and then moving on to the strings, brass, and percussion. However, section **B** is considerably longer than section **A** because each instrument, not just each family of instruments, dominates one variation. (See the outline in the multimedia CD guide to the piece.) Britten uses the capabilities of each instrument—its characteristic quality, innate intensity, rhythmic flexibility, and pitch range—to give each variation a different personality.

Section **C** continues to use the melody borrowed from Purcell but differs from sections **A** and **B** in its form. It is not a theme and variations. Rather, the instruments that play the theme overlap and interweave, creating a *polyphonic* (many-voiced) texture. At times, the Purcell melody can be heard moving systematically from instrument to instrument, piling up in a form called a *fugue*. The fugue offers Britten a chance to juxtapose the various instruments while continuing to use the common thread of the Purcell theme to provide a sense of continuity that unifies the piece.

Throughout *The Young Person's Guide,* Britten portrays the personalities of the various instruments, thereby helping the listener understand that the orchestra is comprised of instrumental families. Much of the work's significance is pedagogical: the composer is seeking to create in the listener's ear a particular perception of the orchestra. Each instrument also relates in characteristic ways to the other instruments in its family. At the same time, each family of instruments serves a different function within the orchestra, which as a whole is a tightly coordinated ensemble. The listener who grasps some of these nuances and can hear aspects of instrumentation has indeed learned a great deal from Britten—and has begun a deeper process of internalizing some important interrelationships of the Western orchestral music soundscape.

Britten presents a common, insider's classification of the Western orchestra as divided into four main sections—strings, woodwinds, brass, and percussion. (See also **"Sound Sources: Voices and Instruments"** in chapter 1 and **"Classifying Musical Instruments"** in the appendix.) Most societies classify their instruments in categories that often provide insights into broader patterns well beyond the boundaries of musical life. For instance, technical advances during the industrial revolution brought about physical changes in some instruments. These alterations affected the sound of the late nineteenth century symphony orchestra, the predecessor of Britten's orchestra. So the very sound of this ensemble is bound up with the history and broader culture of the society from which it came. It has also been suggested that the combination of sixty or more skilled musicians playing together in a musical ensemble resemble the way in which highly skilled workers cooperate in industrial or factory settings.

LISTEN TO the qualities of the various instruments and how the theme is stated and then varied. When is a single instrument especially prominent, and when is an entire family of instruments heard as a unit? Consider the four characteristics of sound. Which instruments can best play sustained pitches and which can produce quick-moving rhythms? How are changes in intensity used to heighten contrasts between instrumental families? When are the pitches of the main theme being stated exactly, and when are they slightly altered?

CASE STUDY:

A un giro sol

A un giro sol by the composer Claudio Monteverdi (1567–1643) recalls a very different soundscape from that of *The Young Person's Guide*. To immerse ourselves in this soundscape, we need to journey back some four hundred years to northern Italy in the late Renaissance and consider how we must change our perspective to make that trip. Only after we have examined the context of *A un giro sol*'s creation can we even begin to imagine how the work was viewed in its day.

    A un giro sol is a *madrigal,* one of a new style of song that emerged in sixteenth-century Italy. Originating in 1520s Florence and Rome, madrigals are short, secular pieces composed for a small group of singers. They are often performed *a cappella,* that is, by voices alone, though some after around 1600 have used instrumental accompaniment. Most madrigals contain four or five vocal lines (three and six or more are also common) that interweave to create a light, poly-phonic texture. Madrigals spread across northern Italy and by the 1540s were performed one-on-a-part by amateur singers who gathered in private homes to sing for an evening.

From the beginning, though, some madrigals were composed for public per-formance; thus madrigals could serve as *incidental music* between acts of a play or as ceremonial music to celebrate a wedding. Since they were to be sung by pro-fessional musicians, these festive public madrigals could be written in a more elaborate or virtuosic vocal style than pieces composed for amateurs.

By the 1580s and 1590s, madrigal composers hoped to move audiences emo-tionally and spiritually by composing music that intensified the emotions por-trayed in the song texts. Composers in the late sixteenth century chose texts by famous poets that evoked strong passions: loneliness, ecstasy, love, fear of death. By the final decades of the century, many madrigals were being composed for entertainment at the major courts of northern Italy. Monteverdi and some of his contemporaries expanded the traditional musical language of the madrigal in order to portray these feelings by, for instance, writing unusual harmonies to evoke feelings of sadness and pain. Four of Monteverdi's eight books of madri-gals, including *A un giro sol,* were published during his two-decade tenure at the Mantuan court.

A un giro sol was published in 1603 but was probably composed several years earlier. It is in five parts, called (from top to bottom) *canto, quinto, alto, tenor,* and *basso.* At the beginning of *A un giro sol,* only three of these voices are heard: the bass sings a descending line on long, sustained notes to provide a foundation while the top two voices, the *canto* and the *quinto,* sing an ornate setting of words "A un giro sol" ("at a turning glance"). The duet in the two upper voices provides us with a fine example of *text-painting;* that is, portraying the words literally in the music, in this case, the lover's bright eyes. The second line of text, which is translated "the breeze laughs all about," is also illustrated in the musical setting: a quick, laugh-like melody appears first in the tenor and then in the alto, then in the canto and in the quinto. (The bass continues to provide stability by singing longer notes, alternating between only two pitches.) In the third line of text, we find a musical shift, as "the sea" is portrayed by a gently undulating melody in the top three voic-es. This lull is itself interrupted by "the wind," in which the tenor runs up and down five notes of a scale; this "wind" phrase is shortly imitated in the upper three voices as well.

TEXT: *A un giro sol*

A un giro sol de' bell' occhi lucenti,	At a single turning glance from those bright eyes
Ride l'aria d'intorno	the breeze laughs all about,
E'l mar s'acqueta e i venti	the sea becomes calm, then the wind dies away
E si fa il ciel d'un altro lume adorno;	and the sky becomes more radiant.
Sol io le luci ho lagrimose e meste.	I alone am sad and weeping.
Certo quando nasceste,	Doubtless on the day you were born,
Cosí crudel e ria,	so cruel and wicked,
Nacque la morte mia.	my death was also born.

At the midpoint of the poem, after line four, the mood shifts suddenly. Where the first half of the text emphasizes light, happy flirtations with turning glances, bright eyes, wind, and water, the second half is considerably more gloomy. The musical setting at the beginning of line five capitalizes on this change in mood. On the word "Sol" ("Alone"), a slower, *homophonic* texture appears as all the voices, briefly led by the bass "alone," state the text together on a new chord that seems surprisingly out of place. But the most vivid feature of this piece comes with the setting of lines six and seven. Note that the tenor and alto sing the text "doubtless on the day you were born" in a perfect unison. But on the second syllable of the seventh line, "so cruel and wicked," this unison shatters as one voice moves up just a half-step to create a *dissonance,* a biting harmony. The sharp dissonance on the text "so cruel and wicked" reflects Monteverdi's desire, shared by many of his contemporaries, to create music that really conveys and augments the emotional content of the text.

Today, sixteenth- and seventeenth-century madrigals are still sung for entertainment and are still valued for their expressive qualities. They can be heard in concerts performed by small choirs, or they may be sung by small groups of accomplished amateurs in more private settings. Indeed, with the growth of the so-called early music movement in the second half of their twentieth century (see chapter 4), the madrigal has enjoyed a "renaissance" of its own as it has more regularly contributed to concert programs and entered the public's musical consciousness. In a way, then, madrigals are once again part of everyday life for many performers and listeners.

LISTEN TO the multivoiced texture and compare it with the texture of the Italian folksong *Vuoi tu venire in Merica.* Does the difference in the textures of the two songs affect the comprehensibility of their texts? Does one of the two textures allow for greater expressiveness?

ADDITIONAL IMPORTANT TERMS

a cappella	incidental music	polyphony
fugue	madrigal	theme
hornpipe	melody	theme and variation form

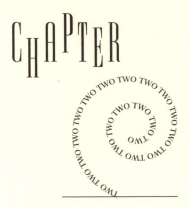

Music of Everyday Life

While we are accustomed to hearing Western classical music in a formal concert hall with an audience sitting in reverent silence, the music in fact originated in many different settings. Much of Western classical music has its roots in liturgy, and throughout its history has been performed at life cycle events such as weddings and funerals. Other music was written for marches and parades; still other pieces accompanied dance. Western classical music today continues to be used for many everyday contexts, such as Muzak, television commercials, and movie soundtracks. For this chapter, keep a diary of all the Western classical music you hear within the course of a twenty-four-hour period. Be sure to take into account the full range of settings in which Western music is played, which extend far beyond the concert hall!

Classical music may serve a wide variety of functions within various social and personal situations but it also reflects the composer's unique set of life experiences and influences. Some composers sought to express both experiences and ideas through their works. For example, expressing the emotions portrayed in a text was one of the primary musical goals of Monteverdi and other composers of the late Renaissance.

But what exactly does it mean to "express" everyday experiences or ideas in music? In this chapter, we will study *Spring,* a concerto from Antonio Vivaldi's *The Four Seasons,* and an excerpt from Gustav Mahler's symphonic song cycle, *The Song of the Earth.* Both compositions speak to aspects of everyday life, one by alluding to nature, the other by describing an everyday scene. As we examine the

8

specific historical circumstances in which these works were created, we will see that our understanding of them has changed since they were composed. Each generation of listeners—indeed, each listener—brings a different perspective, so the reception of both works has undergone drastic changes.

CASE STUDY:

Spring from *The Four Seasons*, First Movement

Despite its declining political power, Venice in the early eighteenth century remained a city in which Western classical music was an essential aspect of everyday life. With its array of important musical institutions, the city and its composers set the standard across Europe for the latest styles in this music. Venice had long been a congenial home for a number of classical soundscapes, including opera, which had played a central role in Venetian society since the 1637 Venice opening of the world's first public opera house. In another domain, St. Mark's Basilica was a center for church music that was widely celebrated in the sixteenth century, long before Monteverdi's tenure as choirmaster there. Later in the seventeenth century, Venetian girls' orphanages that were affiliated with local *ospedali* (charitable institutions) became influential centers of music education. For nearly thirty years, beginning in 1703, the composer Antonio Vivaldi (1678–1741) worked at one such outstanding institution, the *Ospedale della Pietà*. There, his duties included teaching violin and viola as well as conducting and composing intrumental works. It was in this context that Vivaldi composed *The Four Seasons* in the mid-1720s.

The Four Seasons is a set of four works for solo violin and orchestra, known in Italian as *concerti* (singular *concerto,* from an Italian word meaning "to harmonize"). These *concerti* are quite typical of Vivaldi's concerto style and of other works from the period in that they feature a dialogue, with passages alternating between the soloist and the full orchestra. The orchestra plays a catchy theme at the outset, called a *ritornello* (from the Italian word "to return"), setting the mood for the piece and presenting a musical idea that returns frequently throughout the rest of the movement. The soloist's part, in contrast to the ritornello, is much more technically challenging and allows for a show of musical skill.

The riotornello form is commonly heard in concerti from Vivaldi's time. Repeating musical material is the most common and the simplest way to create a form, or structure, for a piece of music.

The Four Seasons is unusual among instrumental compositions of its time because it is *program music,* that is, each of the four concerti illustrates a program, or story—in this case, one explicitly presented in an accompanying poem. (In contrast to program music, *absolute music* is purely abstract, making no such allusions to nonmusical ideas.) The anonymous Italian sonnet, possibly written by Vivaldi himself, was printed throughout the violin part in the original music in order to link each bit of text with its particular musical expression. The first eight lines of the sonnet (which is not sung) are associated with the first movement of the concerto, *Spring:*

SONNET TEXT IN *SPRING*, FIRST MOVEMENT

Giunt'è la Primavera e festosetti,	Joyful Spring has arrived,
La salutan gl'augei con lieto canto,	the birds greet it with their cheerful song,
E i fonti allo spirar de'zeffiretti	and the brooks in the gentle breezes
Con dolce mormorio scorrono intanto.	flow with a sweet murmur.
Vengon' coprendo l'aer di nero amanto	The sky is covered with a black mantle,
E lampi, e tuoni ad annuntiarla eletti	and thunder and lightning announce a storm.
Indi tacendo questi, gl'augelletti;	When they fall silent, the birds
Tornan' di nuovo allor canoro incanto.	take up again their melodious song.

The first movement begins with a statement by the full orchestra of the *ritornello* theme, which appears with the text "joyful spring has arrived." Its mood portrays the springtime theme of the concerto, with a *tempo* (pace) marked "Allegro," literally, cheerful, or merry. After the ritornello, the first section for violin solo begins with a "bird-call" melody consisting mainly of a series of *trills* (fast alternations between two pitches) and quick descending scales; this section corresponds to the text "the birds greet it with their cheerful song." The violin solo is accompanied only by two other violins, which likewise imitate birds. The section ends when the full orchestra returns with a shortened version of the ritornello, itself interrupted by a gently flowing series of trills representing the gurgle of the brook mentioned in lines 3–4. After this tune is presented, the interrupted ritornello is completed at the mid-point of the movement.

The second half of this movement, like its counterpart in the madrigal *A un giro sol* discussed in chapter 1, presents a sudden shift in mood. All the violins play a stormy series of quickly repeated notes low in their range followed by a rapidly ascending scale to represent the "lightning and thunder" of lines 5–6, introducing a section in which elaborate solo passages alternate with stormy grumblings in the orchestra. Eventually, the ritornello returns, only to be interrupted by a new solo section illustrating lines 7–8 of the sonnet, "When they fall silent, the birds / take up again their melodious song." The soloist begins this section with a melody that slowly climbs to a sustained trill; the other violins then enter and imitate the soloist to create an effect of a chorus of bird song. The interrupted ritornello soon resumes. Although all the text of the poem has been used, one more solo section is added to give the soloist a final chance to display his or her virtuosity; finally, a closing section by the orchestra and soloist recalls the opening ritornello theme and reminds the listener of the mood established at the outset.

Although Vivaldi spent most of his life in Venice, his music was very popular across western Europe. *The Four Seasons,* for example, was dedicated to a Bohemian count who was Vivaldi's long-standing *patron* (sponsor). The works were published in Amsterdam in 1725 and soon spread to France, where a so-called Vivaldi fever swept that country in the 1730s. From Bohemia to Amsterdam to Paris, Vivaldi and his Venetian style remained popular for much of the century, as evidenced by the publication of three later arrangements of *The Four Seasons* for other instruments, including one for unaccompanied flute.

Spring can be counted among the "greatest hits" of the eighteenth century, enhancing the cultural landscape of everyday life across Europe. Though Vivaldi's music was generally forgotten throughout the nineteenth century, it was rediscovered early in the twentieth and a wide variety of Vivaldi recordings appeared after World War II.

Today, *The Four Seasons* retains much of the popularity and wide appeal that it saw in the years after its composition. The concerti have appeared on compact disc compilations of classical music's greatest hits, on traditional concert programs, and on television as background music to set a certain ambiance for a luxury car commercial. In today's world, Vivaldi's *Four Seasons* is frequently encountered as a part of everyday musical life.

LISTEN FOR the musical interpretation of the poem. Why do you think these concerti have found a wide audience today? In any way, do they evoke eighteenth-century Venice, the setting from which they originated? Does their use of an "everyday" program explain their accessbility?

CASE STUDY:

Of Youth from *The Song of the Earth*

If Vivaldi's *Spring* has appealed across boundaries of time and culture, Gustav Mahler drew on resources from different cultures to universalize his own feelings about the fleeting nature of life.

Gustav Mahler (1850–1911) composed *The Song of the Earth* (*Das Lied von der Erde*) in the final three years of his life. These were turbulent times for Mahler. As a Jew from Bohemia who converted to Roman Catholicism, he had faced sharp criticism from reviewers while he built a career as a composer and conductor throughout central and eastern Europe. And although Mahler was praised by many for his insightful interpretations during the ten years he directed the Vienna Opera, the conservative, anti-Semitic Viennese press usually condemned his aesthetic choices, both as a conductor and as a composer. When the press argued in 1907 that Mahler's negligence was causing box-office receipts to fall and production expenses to rise, Mahler resigned, saying simply, "All things have their day and I have had mine and so has my work as the local opera director."

The year 1907 was particularly trying for Mahler on other counts as well. In January, he was diagnosed with a defective heart valve that would ultimately prove fatal. Mahler's doctor could only advise him to avoid overexerting himself (penicillin, which came many years later, would have cured him). In June, Mahler was further devastated by the death of his five-year-old daughter, Maria, who succumbed to scarlet fever and diphtheria after a sudden and painful illness of two weeks. Those stressful days and the trauma of losing a child could easily have worsened Mahler's heart condition.

In the weeks following this last disaster, Mahler tried to distract himself by reading *The Chinese Flute*, an anthology of poetry by the ancient Chinese poet Li Tai Po, translated into German and interpreted by Hans Bethge. The poems provided some consolation for Mahler by balancing pessimism with a Dionysian surrender to the pleasures of the world; reading them also moved Mahler into a different cultural domain. Within a year, he began setting some of the poems to music, deciding to build them into "a symphony in six movements for contralto (or baritone), tenor and orchestra."

Each of the six movements that comprise *The Song of the Earth* sets a distinctive mood. In general, Mahler sought to evoke China by writing melodies based on a *pentatonic* scale. This sound, which vaguely resembles some Asian pitch systems and had by Mahler's day come to signal an "exotic" setting outside the West, helps unify the set of songs. Each movement expresses experiences and emotions that Mahler knew intimately. The profound disillusionment with life that Mahler must have felt upon losing his daughter and realizing that his own health was declining is summed up in the refrain of the first movement, "Life is dark, and so is death." The second movement, titled "The Lonely One in Autumn," continues the themes of isolation and loneliness. Where Vivaldi portrayed nature in *The Seasons*, Mahler conveyed a more human experience: feeling the passage of time through a Westerner's idyllic, wistful portrayal of the East.

Of Youth (Von der Jugend), the third song in the cycle and the case study for this chapter, sets a much lighter mood.

TEXT OF *OF YOUTH* (*VON DER JUGEND*):

Mitten in dem kleinen Teiche	In the middle of the little pool
steht ein Pavillon aus grünem	stands a pavilion of green
und aus weissem Porzellan.	and of white porcelain.
Wie der Rücken eines Tigers	Like the back of a tiger
wölbt die Brücke sich aus Jade	the bridge of jade arches
zu dem Pavillon hinüber.	over to the pavilion.
In dem Häuschen sitzen Freunde,	In the little house, friends are sitting
schön gekleidet, trinken, plaudern,	beautifully dressed, drinking, chatting;
manche schreiben Verse nieder.	several are writing verses.
Ihre seidnen Ärmel gleiten	Their silken sleeves slip
rückwärts, ihre seidnen Mützen	backward, their silken caps
hocken lustig tief im Nacken.	perch gaily on the back of their necks.
Auf des kleinen Teiches stiller	On the little pool's still
Wasserfläche zeigt sich alles	surface everything appears
wunderlich im Spiegelbilde.	fantastically in a mirror image.
Alles auf dem Kopfe stehend	Everything is standing on its head
in dem Pavillon aus grünem	in the pavilion of green
und aus weissem Porzellan;	and of white porcelain;
wie ein Halbmond scheint die Brücke	like a half-moon stands the bridge,
umgekehrt der Bogen.	upside-down its arch.
Freunde, schön gekleidet,	Friends, beautifully dressed, are
trinken, plaudern.	drinking, chatting.

The orchestration delicately balances instrumental colors against the voice of the singer, a tenor. Mahler's setting of the first two stanzas sketches a scene—a pavilion in the middle of a small, calm pond—by means of a dialogue between the tenor and the woodwinds, dominated by the flute and the piccolo.

The cellos and trumpet interrupt a repetition of the main melody to announce the beginning of the third stanza, which brings people into the natural scene. Here Mahler changes the orchestration and texture, and shifts the harmony. He intensifies the melody by giving it to the violins and adding active accompaniment by the violas and clarinets. He also gives the tenor a new, contrasting melodic idea, based on a different pentatonic scale, that is repeated in the fourth stanza. The fifth stanza, which describes the "fantastic mirror image" on the surface of the water, expands the new musical idea. The melody and harmony wander about until the development of these ideas is cut short by the flute and oboe playing the original motive. The final two stanzas, set very much like the first two, display subtle changes to the melodic shape that allow the piece to come to a close.

The Song of the Earth deals musically with basic themes of natural and human life cycles that must have been on Mahler's mind when he was composing this work. Nature, idyllically represented and transposed to a Chinese setting in *Of Youth,* contrasted greatly with the turmoil in Mahler's own life, although his illness had not curtailed his own experiences of nature. Yet, however much of Mahler's experiences are expressed in *The Song of the Earth,* the work has during the course of a century transcended its personal expression and moved across cultural boundaries to bring consolation to many.

LISTEN FOR the return of the main melody in verses six and seven, which rounds out the form of the song *Of Youth*. Listen for subtle changes in the melody that bring the piece to a close. Does the repetition of the opening section at the end of the song create a musical analogue of the "mirror-image" discussed in the poem?

ADDITIONAL IMPORTANT TERMS

allegro	ritornello
concerto (pl., concerti)	tempo
patron	trills
program music	pentatonic

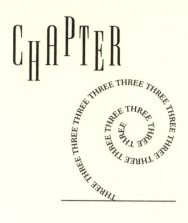

CHAPTER

THREE

Music and

Migration

More and more, European classical music has grown far beyond Europe's borders to become a global style practiced across the Americas, Africa, Asia, and the Pacific. This growth has both resulted from and caused further interchanges between Western and other musical traditions throughout history. Therefore, whether we look at the distant past or at the present, we must understand Western classical music as part of the broader world of music, as a regional musical tradition that has migrated at many points over the course of time, with resulting global contacts and influences.

Here we will explore two relevant examples: one is a composition that emerged from Czech composer Antonín Dvořák's encounter with the New World; the second, a piece by the Polish-French musician Fryderyk Chopin, was among the first Western compositions heard in Japan. The composers of these works had two very different experiences as travelers transplanted into new cultural and social situations. Nevertheless, each had an influence that transcended national and cultural boundaries. Both Dvořák and Chopin contributed to the migration of Western classical music to a new land. (Chopin migrated to Paris, from where his works spread around the world.) As unofficial musical ambassadors from eastern Europe, they furthered the spread both of their native musics and of the "foreign" traditions they encountered in their second countries.

CASE STUDY:

Symphony From the New World

On September 26, 1892, Antonín Dvořák sailed into New York Harbor for the first time, accompanied by his wife and two children. Like others before them, the great Czech composer and his family were awestruck when they saw the towering Statue of Liberty and the sprawling city of New York. On the one hand, Dvořák had the same feelings of strangeness and bewildered astonishment that were— and are—part of every immigrant's experience. On the other, Dvořák's disorientation and anxiety were eased because he was coming on a temporary basis to a well-paying job as director of the recently founded National Conservatory of Music in New York. But where his experience may have resembled that of the transplanted Chinese sojourners discussed in chapter 3, he arrived with much better prospects than most other sojourners: he had already earned a reputation as an outstanding composer and more than thirty performances of his works, in New York, Boston, and Chicago, had preceded him.

For Dvořák, New York in 1892 was a complex mix of alien sights, sounds, and people. East Seventeenth Street in Manhattan, where Dvořák and his family rented a modest but comfortable apartment, was in a relatively genteel neighborhood whose residents were largely middle class and of Dutch, German, Irish, or Slavic descent; the writers William Dean Howells and Herman Melville were among his neighbors. Dvořák enjoyed shopping at the large department stores on the West Side and reading newspapers at any of several cafés closer to home. But he also visited some of the grittier parts of New York, ever a city of sharp contrasts. The Lower East Side was densely packed with Jewish immigrants from eastern Europe and Russia, where just one block housed 39 tenements, 2,781 people, and just 264 toilets.[1] Indeed, lower Manhattan on the East Side was a veritable Tower of Babel, where a visitor could hear Yiddish spoken on one block and Italian, Ukrainian, Chinese, German, or black vernacular spoken on the next. Across town, West Twenty-Eighth Street was developing into Tin Pan Alley, a street filled with shops selling sheet music (printed music of individual popular songs) to be sung and played at home. The sights and sounds of the crossroads that was New York made a lasting impression on the composer.

Dvořák quickly became a part of the elite music scene, earning praise as a teacher, conductor, and composer. His performances with the New York Philharmonic at the new Music Hall on Fifty-Seventh Street (soon to be renamed Carnegie Hall) were widely acclaimed. Dvořák also made a deep impression on his students at the

National Conservatory, which had been founded in 1885 by Jeannette M. Thurber. The conservatory was extraordinarily progressive in admitting talented immigrants, people of color, and women in addition to the affluent white males that comprised the student bodies of other conservatories at the time. Several of Dvořák's students left their marks on him, too: the African American singer and composer Harry T. Burleigh, for example, impressed Dvořák with his sincere interpretations of spirituals.

In January of 1893, Dvořák began working on his Ninth Symphony, which he completed on May 24 and later called *From the New World*. Within days, he departed for the Great Plains, to spend the summer in Spillville, Iowa, a small town with many Czech immigrants. There is some evidence that while in Iowa, Dvořák heard music of various American Indians. After his return to New York, his *New World Symphony* was premiered by the New York Philharmonic at Carnegie Hall on December 16, 1893, with the Austro-Hungarian Anton Seidl conducting.

In a *New York Herald* article that appeared on the day before the symphony's premiere, Dvořák explained the influences that contributed to the composition of this work.

> Since I have been in this country I have been deeply interested in the national music of the Negroes and the Indians. The character, the very nature of a race is contained in its national music. For that reason my attention was at once turned in the direction of these native melodies. I found that the music of the two races bore a remarkable similarity to the music of Scotland. In both there is a peculiar [pentatonic] scale. . . .

> Now, I found that the music of the Negroes and of the Indians was practically identical. I therefore carefully studied a certain number of Indian melodies which a friend gave me, and became thoroughly imbued with their characteristics—with their spirit, in fact.

> It is this spirit which I have tried to reproduce in my new Symphony. I have not actually used any of the melodies. I have simply written original themes embodying the peculiarities of the Indian music, and, using these themes as subjects, have developed them with all the resources of modern rhythms, harmony, counterpoint and orchestral color. . . .

> The second movement is an Adagio [he labeled it "Largo" everywhere else]. . . . It is in reality a study or sketch for a longer work, either a cantata or opera which I propose writing, and which will be based upon Longfellow's "Hiawatha." I have long had the idea of someday utilizing that poem. I first became acquainted with

it about thirty years ago through the medium of a Bohemian translation. It appealed very strongly to my imagination at the time, and the impression has only been strengthened by my residence here.[2]

At least two ideas in this excerpt must be critically examined. First, the composer's assertions about African American and American Indian musics are gross oversimplifications and generalizations. It is unclear how much exposure Dvořák had to Native American music by the time he composed the Symphony. Aside from the encounter in Spillville, most evidence suggests that he had seen only a few transcribed melodies, probably quite inaccurate, and had not heard any live performances, with the possible exception of a visit to Buffalo Bill's Wild West Show. The pentatonic scale that Dvořák claims as a common thread uniting the African American and Native American traditions with the music of Scotland is in fact the very same scale that Mahler used to evoke China in his *Song of the Earth*. While Dvořák may not have been a seasoned expert on American folk idioms, he did subscribe to a time-honored European tradition of using pentatonic themes to represent the exotic "other."

A further influence mentioned by Dvořák is Longfellow's epic poem *The Song of Hiawatha*, which became a best-seller shortly after its publication in 1855 and, as Dvořák notes, impressed him earlier when he read it in a Czech translation. The poem itself is based on an unusual combination of collected legends from American Indian and Finnish sources. Exactly which parts of *Hiawatha* provided the program for the second movement of the Symphony is a subject of some debate, though the two most likely passages describe Hiawatha wooing his future wife Minnehaha and Minnehaha's funeral. In any case, Dvořák clearly used *Hiawatha* to give the work a programmatic and—in his view American—character.

Of the *New World Symphony's* four movements, we will focus on the second, titled *Largo* (very slow, from the Italian word meaning "broad"), which is written in **ABA** form. The **A** section begins with a brief introduction by the orchestral brass. Almost immediately, we hear a simple pentatonic melody played by the English horn (a double-reed woodwind instrument) with sparse accompaniment from the strings. (Some have interpreted this tune as "Hiawatha's wooing.") Although the melody has a narrow range and simple contour that sounds like a "folk tune," Dvořák notes that he composed it himself. It is ironic that this melody, which became widely known in the twentieth century under the title *Goin' Home,* influenced the New World Dvořák meant it to portray: it is often included in American and Canadian funeral services. After the first statement by the English horn, a brief interlude follows in which the woodwinds and brass introduce a *modulation* (change of key). The melody is then repeated, in a new key, and is slightly developed by the violins before the English horn returns, restating the original melody yet again, this time back in the original key.

The **B** section introduces a new melody, in a minor mode, that is stated first by the flutes and oboes together. The melody, which features a slightly faster pace and more complex rhythm than the first melody, is often said to represent Minnehaha's funeral because of its perceived mournful quality. A new, slower-moving theme follows, played by the clarinets and accompanied by pizzicato (plucked, rather than bowed) string basses. After the clarinet theme is stated, the "funeral" melody reappears in the violin section and the two melodies are interwoven and developed in the remainder of the **B** section.

A theme in the oboe begins a transition that leads to a *fanfare* (a short theme meant to signal or call people to attention) by the trumpets, and the end of the **B** section. The English horn restates the original "wooing" melody, just as it did at the beginning of the movement. As in the original **A** section, the tune is passed to the violin section next. The music takes on a quieter, motionless quality as the melody pauses several times and the volume decreases at the end.

As we have seen, Dvořák's Symphony *From the New World* was created by a Czech composer who traveled to New York and tried to incorporate the "spirit" of native American musics into his work. The finished work in fact reflected a variety of influences, including American poetry and European classical music. The pentatonic melodic material represented native America for Dvořák, though to modern ears, the form and style of the work betray the composer's firm grounding in the European musical heritage. The *New World Symphony* intricately interweaves these cultural currents to produce music that, odd as it may seem, helped define Americans' concept of what their music should sound like.

LISTEN as the music gets quieter and slower near the end of the movement and gradually rises to a very soft, high, and sustained chord, which is followed by two final chords played quietly by the string basses.

CASE STUDY:

Chopin's *Polonaise*, op. 53, and Western Music in Japan

In Dvořák's Symphony, we see a single composition that treated foreign elements (as perceived by the composer) within an essentially European musical language.

In this next case study, we examine a much larger process: the wholesale importation of European music to Japan. The *Polonaise* op. 53 by Fryderyk Chopin is significant for two reasons: first, because it is representative of the musical culture, including Chopin's compositions, that was adopted in Japan in the late nineteenth and early twentieth centuries; and second, because Chopin was himself an emigrant from Poland to France. The Japanese appropriation of Western music at the time was part of a broader process of technological and cultural assimilation that had profound effects on Japanese life throughout the twentieth century.

A very brief overview of Japanese history will help us understand the setting and the conditions that triggered this process. Although Western music was probably first heard in Japan when Portuguese traders and missionaries arrived in 1542, the shoguns who ruled Japan imposed a strict policy of seclusion in the mid-seventeenth century. Japanese contact with Europeans was limited to a Dutch trading post at Nagasaki, and for several centuries, Japanese culture was shielded from that of Europe and the rest of the outside world. By the 1850s, it had become obvious that the policy was excluding Japan from the economic boom that resulted from the Industrial Revolution. With the 1854 opening of international ports at Yokohama and Kobe, Western influence increased dramatically. After the shogun feudal system collapsed, the Emperor's new government invited experts from Europe and America to help formulate new and liberal national policies in a wide array of fields. With the institution of this "Meiji Restoration" in 1868, Japan saw a new era of development and modernization.

Musically, the impact of this dramatic policy shift was felt most immediately in the areas of military music and church music. Beginning in the 1850s, the military imported both weapons and training methods from the West, including fife-and-drum bands used in training. By 1871, the Japanese Navy had a thirty-six piece ensemble, including brass, winds, and drums, that was modeled on the English band. An Army band soon followed, and the two groups performed a repertory of primarily Western music at both military and civilian functions. After 1872, when the ban on Christianity was lifted, another Western musical genre took root in Japan. Within only two years, six new hymnals had been published in Japanese, with music based on hymns familiar to the French missionaries who had begun their work in Japan. As Christianity spread, Japanese followers were, for the first time, singing music of Western origin.

Although hymns and military Western music quickly found a place within Japanese culture, the assimilation of Western classical music was a more gradual but more far-reaching process. In Japan today, there are at least twenty-four professional symphony orchestras, nine of which are based in Tokyo alone. Dozens of foreign orchestras visit Japan each year. Two major national opera companies perform Western operas regularly. On any given night in Tokyo, a concertgoer can choose from more than twenty performances featuring classical Western programs. And the Japanese people not only listen to Western music, they perform it as well: some 200 amateur orchestras and over 15,000 amateur choirs rehearse and perform in Japan. So Western classical music, which comprises only a small share of the American commercial music market, plays a substantial role in Japan.

How did the Western classical tradition come to occupy such a central place in Japanese culture? The authorities during the reign of the Meiji Emperor (1867–1912) certainly did not encourage adopting Western classical music for aesthetic reasons. Rather, the Western musical system found its place in Japan first as an educational tool and only later as an art form per se. An essential element in the Meiji Reformation was the establishment of new uniform standards for education, so the government called on experts familiar with the Dutch and French educational systems to provide a model. The first set of regulations on education, written in 1872, included singing and playing musical instruments as part of the elementary and middle-school curricula, but Japan lacked both teachers and teaching materials appropriate for the young. For the moment, music education in Japan was nothing more than a good idea.

When the government sent a school principal, Izawa Shuji, to Boston in July 1875 to study elementary schooling, he was hardly expected to return with a plan for music education in Japan. But while studying at the Bridgewater State Normal School and then at Harvard University, Izawa became convinced of the need for music education in his native country. He returned to Japan in 1878, and began to organize the national curriculum for music education. Izawa collaborated with his music tutor from Boston, Luther W. Mason, to draft and implement a "Plan for the Study of Music," which declared that music education should blend "Eastern and Western music [to] establish a kind of music which is suitable for the Japan of today."[3] In 1885, he was appointed director of the newly established Music Study Centre (which later became the Tokyo Music School and moved into the Sogakudo building in Ueno Park, Tokyo, where it stands today).

The Music Study Centre developed a curriculum that included Western music theory, singing, and playing piano, organ, and violin, as well as Japanese instruments. Izawa and Mason worked to transcribe and compile Japanese children's songs along with excerpts from Western compositions and popular music for use as an introductory textbook, while the Centre (and later the Music School) trained teachers who would take this new curriculum into classrooms across Japan. As generation after generation of students were introduced to Western music through this curriculum, Western classical music gradually came to occupy its present prominent position in Japan.

On February 20, 1886, the Study Centre held its first graduation concert. The program featured the new graduates performing a polonaise by Fryderyk Chopin (1810–1849), several Japanese songs, two piano pieces by the German composer Carl Maria von Weber, a string quartet by Joseph Haydn, and vocal pieces by Haydn and Beethoven sung with Japanese lyrics and orchestral accompaniment. This eclectic program reflects the spirit of the new Japanese musical culture that Izawa and Mason intended. Not only were performances given in "purely" Western and Japanese genres, but the two cultures were fused to create something entirely new.

Sadly, we don't know which polonaise by Chopin was performed at the concert, but the choice of composer is oddly fitting. Chopin, an 1831 emigrant from Warsaw to Paris, evoked his own Polish musical tradition as he composed for a broader European audience, weaving together different musical cultures, much as Izawa did. Having moved to France at the age of twenty-one, Chopin quickly gained recognition as a composer and pianist, and soon was socializing with the great intellectuals and artists of his time, such as the writers Victor Hugo, Heinrich Heine, and George Sand (Aurore Dudevant, with whom he had a nine-year romance); the artist Eugène Delacroix; and composers Franz Liszt and Hector Berlioz. Although he died young in 1849, he had produced a large corpus of piano works that are still mainstays of the concert pianist's repertory.

The *polonaise* is a stately dance in triple meter that originated as a festive processional piece at seventeenth-century Polish courts. Works in this style were later set by Bach, Handel, Mozart, Beethoven, and other composers, but Chopin reclaimed the form as a symbol of Polish identity, producing sixteen over the course of his life.

Chopin's Polonaise in A-flat major, op. 53, has a broad **ABA** form that is preceded by an introduction featuring quick ascending lines. The recognizable dance tune with its characteristic polonaise rhythm marks the beginning of the **A** section. Note the fast, dramatic and wavelike ascending scales that occur at important points in the course of the piece. One such scale heralds the return of the original idea with the polonaise rhythm, this time with the addition of an extra ornament. Another introduces a contrasting theme based on the same polonaise rhythm but somewhat less lively. Yet another, somewhat shorter, ushers in the return of the original theme, after which the **A** section closes.

The **B** section is introduced by a sudden change in key and six *rolled chords* (where the pitches within each chord are played in quick succession). A four-note pattern that begins in the bass serves as an accompaniment for the first half of the **B** section. A melody appears in the higher registers; it has a flowing quality at first but suggests the polonaise rhythm from time to time. The section gradually builds in intensity to a climax, only to start over again very quietly. The second time around, the music accelerates gradually to create a feeling of quiet intensity. When the four-note bass line drops out, a new, songlike melody emerges in a new key; another theme succeeds it, subtly moving from one key to another and still another. Finally, we hear the original polonaise motive as the **B** section ends. A somewhat shortened **A** section reiterates the music that appeared at the beginning of the work and brings the piece to a close.

LISTEN TO how the strict rhythm gives way to a freer style, the performer speeding up or slowing down to create tension or to emphasize a particular part of a melody. Listen also for the sometimes subtle changes in tempo and for the heavy use of ornamentation, another characteristic feature of works by Chopin. Many of his pieces contain fast and intricate passages, requiring great virtuosity to play.

ADDITIONAL IMPORTANT TERMS

English horn	pizzicato
fanfare	polonaise
largo	rolled chord
modulation	sheet music

CHAPTER

FOUR

The Study of Local Music

A musical soundscape is shaped by its setting. Many European and American composers have sought to represent nature, the seasons, or the emotions through song and instrumental works, but some have also embedded the sights and sounds of small towns and urban centers in their music. One remarkable example dating from the Renaissance is *The Cries of London,* a piece for five voices and a consort of viols by Orlando Gibbons (1583–1625). This two-part composition captures the sounds heard on the streets of early seventeenth-century London—such miscellaneous shouts as the town crier proclaiming the time and vendors selling a great variety of goods, including "lily white mussels" and "ripe chestnuts." More recent works that characterize localities in music are twentieth-century compositions that represent two very different places in musical sound. Aaron Copland's *Billy the Kid* reimagines the Old West and Steve Reich's *City Life* depicts the sounds of New York City.

CASE STUDY:
Billy the Kid

A composer who can mirror a well-known musical landscape can also imagine an unfamiliar place. Such is the case with Aaron Copland and his ballet, *Billy the Kid,* which recreates a world that could not be farther from the composer's peri-

24

od, background, or experience. Aaron Copland was born in Brooklyn, New York, in 1900, the son of Russian Jewish immigrants who owned a successful department store. Copland's Brooklyn resembled Dvořák's New York described above in its multi-ethnic makeup. His neighborhood, now called Crown Heights, had many Irish and German immigrants as well as Welsh, Scottish, and Swedish families. Copland's family spoke some Yiddish at home, and Copland was impressed by the Hebrew chant he heard at synagogue and the lively dance music that was played at weddings. In short, his early experience, like Dvořák's more fleeting exposure, included a variety of musical and cultural influences from which he borrowed freely to use in his compositions later in life.

Some of Copland's earlier works borrow heavily from jazz, while others are based on a wide range of American folk tunes. Still other compositions were inspired by his travel to new locales in the Americas, such as *El Salón México,* which he completed in 1936, four years after a visit to a Mexico City dance hall. Using popular tunes culled from a *cancionero mexicano* (a collection of Mexican songs), Copland tried to convey the feel of that dance hall without simply imitating the music he heard there.

> It wasn't so much the music or the dances that attracted me as the spirit of the place. In some inexplicable way, while milling about in those crowded halls, I had felt a live contact with the Mexican "people" . . . their humanity, their shyness, their dignity and unique charm. I remember quite well that it was at such a moment I conceived the idea of composing a piece about Mexico and naming it *El Salón México.* . . . My purpose was not merely to quote [the music] literally, but to heighten without in any way falsifying the natural simplicity of Mexican tunes.[1]

Another popular work by Copland in which he adapts native music to evoke the spirit of a locale is *Appalachian Spring, ballet music* intended to accompany a dance performance. Later arranged as an *orchestral suite* that was not intended for dancing, *Appalachian Spring* borrows the famous Shaker hymn *'Tis a Gift to Be Simple.* Throughout his career, Copland composed in a style that suggested the broad sweep of (usually American) open spaces by relying on "open" harmonies— intervals of fifths and octaves—as well as unusual dance rhythms. Copland's use of well-known folk tunes strongly associated with a particular place also increases the powerful local connections evoked by many of his compositions.

Copland's ballet *Billy the Kid* was suggested by Lincoln Kirstein, the director of a touring dance company called Ballet Caravan. Like the other companies Kirstein founded (including the New York City Ballet in 1948), Ballet Caravan sought to develop a distinctly American style of ballet, not just by employing American dancers and choreographers but also by programming dances based on American themes. Kirstein gave the choreographer Eugene Loring a copy of Walter Noble Burns's *The Saga of Billy the Kid* (1925), with the intention of mounting just such a new ballet. Kirstein passed the resulting ballet scenario on to Copland along with two collections of cowboy tunes. The ballet premiered in Chicago on October 6, 1938, and is still regarded as a good classical-music representation of the American West. The following year, Copland shortened the ballet and rearranged it as an orchestral suite; it is this *concert version* that is used in our case study. Importing music conceived for dancing into a new context— the concert hall—is a longstanding practice (see also the discussion of the new tango, in chapter 6.)

Copland summarizes the plot of his ballet, inspired by Burns's popular work of "historical fiction."

> *Billy the Kid* concerns itself with significant moments in the life of this infamous character of the American Southwest, known to the Mexicans as *El Chivato,* or simply, "The Keed," The ballet begins and ends on the open prairie. The first scene is a street in a frontier town. Cowboys saunter into town, some on horseback, others on foot with lassoes; some Mexican women do a *Jarabe* [a Mexican dance], which is interrupted by a fight between two drunks. Attracted by the gathering crowd, Billy, a boy of twelve, is seen for the first time, with his mother. The brawl turns ugly, guns are drawn, and in some unaccountable way, Billy's mother is killed. Without an instant's hesitation, in cold fury, Billy draws a knife from a cowhand's sheath and stabs his mother's slayers. His short but famous career has begun. In swift succession we see episodes in Billy's later life—at night, under the stars, in a quiet card game with his outlaw friends; hunted by a posse led by his former friend Pat Garrett; in a gun battle. A celebration takes place when he is captured. Billy makes one of his legendary escapes from prison. Tired and worn out in the desert, Billy rests with his girl. Finally the posse catches up with with him.[2]

Locale is an essential part of the plot. Imagine what a different story would result if the first scene were set in Boston—or Venice! The images of sauntering cowboys, life in a small Western town, and a brawl in the street are vividly portrayed in the music. Although he had initially planned to avoid using Kirstein's cowboy melodies, Copland suggests that the tunes became more appealing because of a cross-cultural experience he had in France:

I have never been particularly impressed with the musical beauties of the cowboy song as such. . . . As far as I was concerned, this ballet could be written without benefit of the poverty-stricken tunes Billy himself must have known.

Nevertheless, in order to humor Mr. Kirstein, who said he didn't really care whether I used cowboy material or not, I decided to take his two little collections with me when I left for Paris in the summer of 1938. . . . Perhaps there is something different about a cowboy song in Paris. But whatever the reason may have been, it wasn't very long before I found myself hopelessly involved in expanding, contracting, rearranging and superimposing cowboy tunes on the rue de Rennes in Paris.[3]

The ballet requires a fairly large orchestra that includes a piano and a large number of percussion instruments: timpani, glockenspiel (a metallophone closely related to the xylophone), xylophone, sleigh bells, wood blocks, gourd, snare drum, slapstick, cymbals, bass drum, and triangle. Six borrowed cowboy tunes are woven into the orchestral fabric of the work. We will focus on the first scene of the ballet, *Street in a Frontier Town*, which follows a processional called *The Open Prairie*. The scene can be divided into five major sections.

As the scene opens, the *piccolo* (a small, high-pitched flute) opens with the first cowboy song, *Great Grand-Dad*. When this melody is repeated, it is interrupted by a duet for oboe and trumpet, which clash with each other as they play the refrain, "Whoopee ti yi yo, git along, little dogies" from another cowboy song, *Git Along, Little Dogies*. Because this tune (which, as we see in chapter 8, may derive from Cajun French sources) evokes the sauntering cowboys mentioned by Copland in the plot synopsis, it is a crucial element in fixing the setting: the street of a frontier town. The two melodies are tossed from one instrumental section to another—now in the strings, now in the trombones—as occasional short, percussive outbursts enliven the texture. Eventually, the melodies become distorted and a lopsided dance rhythm emerges. In this pattern, the meter keeps constantly shifting between three-beat and four-beat groupings—triple and quadruple meter—so that the listener has trouble predicting when accented beats will occur. Fragments of *Git Along, Little Dogies* are passed from the violins to the trombones and back again in smaller and smaller segments until finally only one pitch remains of the motive. Suddenly, the full orchestra enters to play an interlude based on a bit of the *Git Along, Little Dogies* melody. As this interlude ends, the second section begins.

The violins now introduce the third cowboy song, *The Old Chisholm Trail*, while the brass and percussion provide an "oom-pah" accompaniment that emphasizes the off-beats. Like the piccolo at the beginning of the scene, the violins repeat the melody, only to be interrupted by another cowboy song, *The Streets of Laredo*, played by the trombones in a triple meter that is superimposed on the quadruple meter maintained by the strings and woodwinds. This combination of tunes has specific geographical connections: the Chisholm Trail, a network of paths used between the 1860s and the 1890s to herd Texas longhorn cattle northward to Kansas and beyond, and Laredo, Texas, a frontier town on the Rio Grande that was one of the trail's southern terminals. *The Old Chisholm Trail* and *The Streets of Laredo* therefore suggest a real geographical setting for the unfolding scene, as do *Git Along, Little Dogies* and *Goodbye Old Paint* (heard in the scene's final section), both of which mention Wyoming. Next *The Old Chisholm Trail* returns, only to get stuck on a little accented three-note idea that is played eight times before the oboes and trumpets enter with the dissonant *Git Along, Little Dogies*.

Now the third section begins, with a return of *Great Grand-Dad* played by the piccolo as the two melodies of the first section are interwoven once again while the violins and piano provide a rhythmic accompaniment. Try to imagine which cowboys are on horseback and which are arriving on foot with lassos, as Copland suggests.

The fourth section of the scene is a jarabe, a Mexican dance in quintuple meter. This unusual pattern consists of alternating groups of two and three beats: ONE-two-THREE-four-five. The woodblock can be heard distinctly on the accented beats (one and three) of each measure. The trumpet carries the jarabe melody while the rest of the orchestra provides the dance rhythm. The quintuple dance rhythm is occasionally interrupted by a measure of quadruple meter that adds another layer of asymmetry, preventing the listener from settling too comfortably into the quintuple rhythm. This asymmetry may reflect the conflicting worlds of the Mexican women who are dancing and the crowd of cowboys who are anticipating a brawl.

With the end of the jarabe, the final section begins as the piece settles into a more stable triple meter and the violins introduce a simple new melody, the refrain of the cowboy song *Goodbye, Old Paint*. The oboe then presents the music of the verse, and the strings return with the refrain, soon to be embellished by the glockenspiel. Gradually, the texture grows thicker and the orchestra gets louder as more instruments join in. The timpani and trombone begin accenting the second beat of each measure, and the trumpets blare the verse, only to be shouted down by the violins playing the refrain in a high register. The brawl begins. The song is now reduced to a new, accented, two-note motive that is repeated, louder and louder, by the strings and woodwinds until the climax, when the slapstick enters for the first time to create the sound of a gunshot. We hear two more emphatic chords and we know that Billy's mother has been killed. After a tense moment, the bass drum, cello, and string bass intone two mournful beats, leading to the next scene.

Copland's *Billy the Kid,* and particularly the scene *Street in a Frontier Town,* is a musical portrait of a romanticized Wild West that has endured in the American imagination. On the one hand, Copland's music reflected a variety of American musics, as he borrowed melodies and stylistic devices from its various idioms. But Copland also created an art music that was American in an unprecedented way. In the spirit of the vision that Dvořák had offered a generation before, Copland defined a new American music fashioned from a fusion of popular-song genres. One essential element in Copland's unique mixture is the representation of particular locales in his works: a "local music" of America was born.

LISTEN FOR the cowboy songs that provide the melodic interest in this composition, noticing the power of these songs to evoke the West through their longtime association and widespread circulation in American oral tradition.

CASE STUDY:
City Life: "Check It Out"

Composers often write about the places they know best, and cities have always been an important part of Steve Reich's experience. Born in New York City in 1936, Reich as a teenager explored a variety of soundscapes; when he was fourteen, for example, he discovered the music of Bach, Stravinsky, and bebop, all of them musics that would influence his later compositions.

In the summer of 1957, Reich, then aged twenty, graduated from Cornell University with a degree in philosophy and returned to New York City. After trying and rejecting the world of academic music and living for a time in San Francisco, Reich pursued new experimental styles, which really interested him. From the 1960s until now, Reich has composed music in which slow changes play a central role. For example, in *Come Out* (1966), Reich used a tape recording of the phrase "come out to show them" that was spoken by a defendant in the politically charged trial of the so-called Harlem Six. In the piece, the tape is duplicated and two tape loops are played, at first in unison, then slipping slowly out of phase to create an echo effect. Over the course of the thirteen-minute work, more copies of the tape are added until eight layers of the loop are playing simultaneously. Since the piece makes use of very little musical material—in this case, only a short loop of tape—

and includes a great deal of repetition, Reich's music has been described as *mini-malist*. Over the years, Reich has drawn on his wide-ranging musical interests, among them jazz, Balinese gamelan, Hebrew chant, and West African drumming, for basic material to be manipulated in this minimalist style.

Reich's experiences as a resident of New York City provided the material for several of his compositions. *Livelihood* (1964) was based on tape recordings of passengers' conversations from the cab that Reich drove at the time. Improvements in audio technology in the 1980s and 1990s offered Reich expanded possibilities as well. One such innovation was the sampler, which records a short sound byte electronically and plays it back on demand.

City Life, dating from 1995, takes advantage of this *sampling* technology, allowing Reich to incorporate sounds from everyday city life into the fabric of a live perfor-mance of a concert piece. Reich recognizes that he is by no means the first person to incorporate sounds from "real life" in a musical setting; for example, he cites George Gershwin's imitation of taxi horns in his orchestral work *An American in Paris* and various songs from the worlds of rock and rap as his precedents. And we may recall the simulated bird song in Vivaldi's *Four Seasons* (see chapter 2 of this booklet).

City Life, a work in five movements, calls for 2 flutes, 2 oboes, 2 clarinets, 2 pianos, 3 (or 4) percussionists, 2 violins, viola, cello, string bass, and 2 sampling key-boards. The samplers contain speech excerpts, car horns, door slams, air brakes, subway chimes, and other sounds. The primary motive in the first movement is derived from a sampled recording of a street vendor in lower Manhattan saying "Check it out."

The movement, which consists of five sections and a short *coda* (concluding section), opens with a slow, homophonic introduction in which woodwinds, strings, and piano play jazzy chords. Section **A** of the movement introduces the quick three-note motive on which the rest of the piece is based. This motive is stated first by two instruments in unison: a piano and a *vibraphone* (an idiophone much like a large xylophone, with a bell-like sound). It is punctuated by sampled sounds, including a door slam and air brakes from a bus and from a subway. The speech sample "Check it out" soon appears, and the texture takes on a more poly-phonic quality as more instruments enter the mix, playing the three-note motive slightly out of sync with the original piano-vibraphone combination. We become aware that the three-note motive played by all these instruments is based on the rhythm and pitch of the words "Check it out." As the texture becomes thicker and more complex, more and more sampled sound effects are added, now including a car motor and a car horn.

The **B** section begins with a striking modulation and an emphatic restatement of the three-note motive along with the speech sample. As the motive is repeated more frequently, the piece takes on a feeling of urgency and the tension builds. A short, accented note in the piano's bass frequently punctuates the motive, almost like an exclamation point, and a cymbal can be heard from time to time.

Another modulation, this time to a minor key, marks the beginning of the **C** section. The woodwinds (flute, oboe, and clarinet) soon add a new layer of long-held chords to the already dense texture. These instruments, imitating a car horn, keep repeating three different chords over and over, changing the rhythm and the order in which they occur. The texture continues to thicken as the cymbal occasionally imitates the sound of the air brakes.

Section **D** modulates yet again, suddenly thinning the texture and slowing the frenzied activity. The motive is *inverted* (turned upside-down) to add a new level of interest. Because of the inversion, the three ascending notes have been transformed into three descending notes. The bass drum imitates the sound of the slamming door, and the piece, haltingly at first, regains momentum. Soon the movement regains its lively, upbeat feeling, which is interrupted by an emphatic "Check it out" in the vibraphones, pianos, and strings, all together.

Section **E** begins here, and the slow, sustained jazz chords from the introduction return. The musical events are now spaced farther apart as the sustained chords become more prominent. Eventually, the sampled sounds and the quick motive drop out altogether, leaving only the sustained, homophonic chords. This final section, which is analogous to the introduction, is called a *coda*, from the Italian word for "tail." The slow chords of the coda eventually lead directly into the second movement of *City Life*.

LISTEN FOR the tire skid in Section **E,** which is imitated immediately by the piano and strings. How many "real-world" sounds of the city can you find in this movement of *City Life*?

ADDITIONAL IMPORTANT TERMS

ballet	*jarabe*	sampling
cancionero	motive	triple, quadruple, and quintuple meter
coda	orchestral suite	vibraphone
inversion	piccolo	

CHAPTER FIVE

Music of Worship
and Belief

In chapter 5, we take a close look at music used for worship. In the case of Tibetan Buddhism, Afro-Cuban Santería, and Ethiopian Christianity, we can trace how an indigenous musical style has been adapted to ritual settings and how the settings, sounds, and significances of these musics have changed to better serve the different belief systems.

Western Christian chant has also adapted to different settings. The chant of the early Church, with its roots in Middle Eastern Jewish liturgical music, later spread throughout the Roman empire. It has been called *Gregorian chant* because Pope Gregory I (590–604) was credited by some with establishing the papal choir and with having put the chants in order for the church liturgy used throughout Europe. But plainchant continued to be influenced from many sources as long as it was transmitted orally. Around the ninth century, during a period of expansion and change, a system of musical notation was developed, allowing people to preserve chant melodies in writing. The notation was made up of *neumes*, marks of various shapes that stand for small groups of pitches.

By around the twelfth century, the form (but not the musical content) of the Mass, the central Christian worship service, had stabilized. The Mass and chants, all in Latin, remained essentially at the center of Christian ritual practice until the 1960s, when the Second Vatican Council discarded the old Latin chants in favor of vernacular musics and languages thought to be more meaningful to people of widely differing cultural backgrounds and localities.

The Mass as performed in the late medieval period consisted of the *Ordinary*, texts that were recited at every service, interspersed with the *Proper*, texts that were chosen to reflect the day's religious observances.

CASE STUDY:
Haec dies (chant)

The text of the Western Christian chant *Haec dies* is taken from the biblical Book of Psalms, verses 106:1 and 118:24. The piece is a *Gradual*, part of the Proper of the Mass recited in the Mass service on Easter Sunday. We will hear two musical settings of this text. The first, a Gregorian chant and the older of the two, can be found in the *Liber Usualis*, a thick book that contains most of the chants currently in use. The text is as follows:

Haec dies	This is the day
quam fecit Dominus	which the Lord hath made;
exsultemus et	we will rejoice and
laetemur in ea.	be glad in it.
Confitemini Domino,	O give thanks to the Lord,
quoniam bonus:	for He is good:
quoniam in saeculum	for forever
misericordia	endureth
ejus.	His mercy.

The musical setting is melismatic, that is, each syllable of the text (with few exceptions) is set to several pitches. These extended syllables, or *melismas,* are drawn out in an especially elaborate manner in order to highlight certain important words, particularly *Dominus* ("the Lord"), *exsultemus* ("we will rejoice"), *saeculum* ("forever") and *ejus* ("His").

The melody, sung by a soloist or *monophonically* in unison by the choir, moves largely by steps and avoids leaps, allowing the psalm text to be easily understood. The vocal range of the chant, just over an octave, is suitable for all singers. Furthermore, the melody tends to hover around just two pitches, a *reciting tone,* on which much of the text is sung, and the *final*, the first and last pitch of the chant. The chant is sung with a free rhythm that emphasizes the connection between speech and song.

LISTEN TO the soloist and choir singing in a call and response form, first encountered in chapter 3, which in chant is termed *responsorial* style. Note that the chant text itself suggests this performance style: The choir sings on the text "we will rejoice" but the soloist sings on the text "O give thanks" (imperative plural).

CASE STUDY:
Haec dies (organum)

An anonymous treatise *Musica enchiriadis* ("Music Handbook"), written around the year 900, heralds a major new development in the music of the church: it uses the term *organum* to describe the addition of a second voice above or below a plainchant melody. In the earliest, simplest types of organum, the second voice sang a line parallel to the chant: that is, the two voices started on different pitches at an interval of a fourth or a fifth apart, and then moved in the same direction at the same time. This simple parallel organum was occasionally modified. When parallel motion would cause an unwanted interval, the second voice could simply stop moving, remaining on a single pitch while the plainchant continued to move. This kind of motion, in which one voice remains on a constant pitch while the other changes pitch, is called *oblique* motion.

By the late twelfth century, composers at the Cathedral of Notre Dame in Paris had brought the technique of organum to a new height. Léonin, a poet and musician who worked at Notre Dame between 1163 and 1190, was widely recognized as the first master of this new style, called *Notre Dame organum*. The principal voice, singing the plainchant melody, was slowed down dramatically so that even a short melodic segment could be drawn out for a long period of time. Meanwhile, the second voice could sing a lively melody above the chant.

LISTEN TO the long-held notes and notice that only the first two words of the chant are sung. The chant is slowed down so much that it may be difficult to hear that the drawn-out melody in the lower voice is actually the chant we just heard. The other voice presents an ornate melody in a rhythm that can be performed in one of a number of ways depending on how the musicians interpret the notation.

CASE STUDY:
Gloria from the Pope Marcellus Mass

A world of difference separates the church music of the late twelfth century, when the organum *Haec dies* was composed, from that of the late sixteenth century, when the *Pope Marcellus* Mass was composed. During those four hundred years, polyphonic music underwent enormous development and change, and the humanist movement transformed the arts, the sciences, and society during the Renaissance. The Low Countries and Italy had become great centers of musical innovation.

Beginning in the fourteenth century, instead of setting only one section of the Mass Ordinary, such as the Kyrie or the Gloria, which would then be combined with other sections to create a complete Ordinary, composers began setting all five movements as a musical unit. By the late 1400s, this development allowed a single melody or motive to be developed throughout the Mass, adding a new dimension of musical unity to the service. Often, a Mass was based on a borrowed melody, such as a Gregorian chant or a popular tune, which was incorporated into the polyphonic fabric of sound. By the sixteenth century, entire polyphonic pieces, such as madrigals, were incorporated into Mass settings, with six, eight, or even more independent voices common in Rome, Venice, and other centers of church music.

Some progressive musicians and critics welcomed these innovations. But more conservative clergy members decided that the complex polyphony and the use of secular melodies and instruments in church distracted worshippers from the religious experience at services. Some of them became especially upset when members of the congregation recognized familiar popular tunes within a Mass and laughed out loud.

The Council of Trent, a group of Church officials, was assembled to reform the abuses and laxity of the Catholic Church. The Council decreed in 1562 that "all music tainted with sensual and impure elements, all secular forms and unedifying language" should be purged from the Church. A committee of eight cardinals was charged with implementing the Council's declarations on church music.

Giovanni Pierluigi da Palestrina was a prominent composer and choirmaster who was known best for his Masses and other sacred works, most of which were composed during his appointments at three of the oldest and most eminent churches in Rome. Palestrina's early Masses, like those of his contemporaries, were based on secular tunes and often featured polyphony that obscured the words being sung. Nevertheless, especially in his later years, Palestrina gained a reputation as the leading musician in his day because his music exhibited a fine, balanced craftsmanship that would serve as a model for future generations.

The *Pope Marcellus* Mass was published in 1567, several years after the committee of cardinals was formed. Although the exact year of its composition is unknown, Palestrina may have written the Mass to conform with Counter-Reformation sensibilities. The *Gloria* of the Mass, which is written for six groups of voices, opens with a single voice performing the first line of the text as plain-chant; on the text "et in terra pax" ("and on earth peace"), four voices enter. The ornaments in the tenor emphasize the words "Laudamus te" ("We praise Thee") and "Benedicimus te" (We bless Thee"). On the text "Adoramus te" (We adore Thee"), the texture is reduced to three voices—only half of the ensemble—as the upper voices drop out, making that line more intimate and personal than what came before. "Glorificamus te" ("We glorify Thee") seems jubilant in comparison as the upper voices return, and "Gratias agimus tibi" ("We give Thee thanks") is sung by five voices, with the soprano suddenly jumping to high notes to "give thanks" enthusiastically. The texture then alternates between three and four voices until "Domine fili" ("O Lord [the only begotten] Son") is repeated for empha-sis, with all six voices singing simultaneously for the first time in the Gloria, with most choir members singing in the high part of their range. The texture thins out to three voices again at "Domine Deus, Agnus Dei" ("Lord God, Lamb of God") in order to portray the "Lamb of God" more tenderly.

As the second section of the *Gloria* begins on the text "Qui tollis" ("Thou that takest away"), the mood changes. "Miserere nobis" ("have mercy on us") is set first in three voices and then in four. When the same text returns four lines later, it is set to a different music but again has a simple three-voice texture. Note the orna-mentation on "Tu solus Dominus" ("Thou only art the Lord") and the full, six-voice homophonic setting of "Jesu Christe." Finally, as the movement comes to a close, the inner voices criss-cross while the sopranos sustain a single long pitch for the beautiful "Amen."

LISTEN TO the homophonic texture of the *Gloria* of this Mass that makes the text easily comprehensible. Note that Palestrina rarely uses all six voices at the same time. By varying the number of voices, he is able to create different textures, to either highlight certain parts of the text or to give the text a more subdued quali-ty. When listening to this Mass movement, take note of these subtle changes in texture.

Gloria in excelsis Deo	Glory be to God on high,
et in terra pax hominibus	and on earth peace to men
bonae voluntatis.	of good will.
Laudamus te.	We praise Thee.
Benedicimus te.	We bless Thee.
Adoramus te.	We adore Thee.
Glorificamus te.	We glorify Thee.
Gratias agimus tibi propter	We give Thee thanks for

magnam gloriam tuam.	Thy great glory.
Domine Deus, Rex caelestis,	Lord God, heavenly King,
Deus Pater omnipotens.	God the Father Almighty.
Domine Fili	O Lord, the only-begotten Son,
unigenite, Jesu Christe.	Jesus Christ.
Domine Deus, Agnus Dei,	Lord God, Lamb of God,
Filius Patris.	Son of the Father.
Qui tollis	Thou that takest away
peccata mundi,	the sins of the world,
miserere nobis.	have mercy on us.
Qui tollis peccata mundi,	Thou that takest away the sins
suscipe deprecationem nostram.	of the world, receive our prayer.
Qui sedes ad dexteram Patris,	Thou that sittest at the right hand
miserere nobis.	of the Father, have mercy on us.
Quoniam tu solus sanctus.	For thou alone art holy.
Tu solus Dominus.	Thou only art the Lord.
Tu solus Altissimus.	Thou alone art most high.
Jesu Christe, cum Sancto Spiritu	Jesus Christ, along with the Holy Spirit
in gloria Dei Patris.	in the glory of God the Father.
Amen.	Amen.

ADDITIONAL IMPORTANT TERMS

final	neumes	parallel motion
melismas	oblique motion	reciting tone
monophony	organum	responsorial

CHAPTER

SIX

Music and Dance

Dances and dance musics have an uncanny ability to cross cultural and geographical boundaries. For example, in chapter 6 we learn that bhangra began as a harvest dance and developed into an international sensation as it spread through South Asian diaspora communities. Similarly, the erotic subtext of the nineteenth-century Argentine tango is the foundation on which the cosmopolitan concert *new tango* has been built. We have already encountered two examples of dances crossing cultural and geographical boundaries: the polonaise, a formal processional in seventeenth-century Polish courts, was later adapted for concert music, and the *jarabe,* a Mexican dance, turned up in Copland's ballet and orchestral suite *Billy the Kid.*

Two dances from the sixteenth century or earlier, the *jig* and the *hornpipe,* both originated in the British Isles. They developed from popular entertainment and were later incorporated into the art music enjoyed by the nobility across Europe. The elite form of the jig, a popular dance among Irish Americans (see chapter 2), is usually called by the French term *gigue* (pronounced "zheeg"). It makes an appearance in a 1707 *suite* (a series of stylized dances grouped as a set) composed for the harpsichord by Elisabeth-Claude Jacquet de la Guerre. The hornpipe, which Benjamin Britten used in his *Young Person's Guide to the Orchestra* (which itself is modeled on a seventeenth-century composition by Henry Purcell), supplies the basis for a section of George Frideric Handel's *Water Music,* a suite for orchestra composed in the early eighteenth century. Throughout most of European history, as all these examples attest, the same dances have been an important part of the musical life in various social and economic settings.

CASE STUDY:

Gigue no. 2 from Jacquet de la Guerre's *Pieces for Harpsichord*, Suite no. 1

The terms *jig* and *gigue* both derive from the French verb *giguer,* meaning "to frolic" or "to leap." *Jig* was used in the British Isles as early as the fifteenth century to describe a popular dance, and by the sixteenth century, it was widely understood as both lively and bawdy, leading Shakespeare to suggest in *Much Ado About Nothing*: "Wooing is hot and hasty like a Scottish jigge." In seventeenth-century England, the jig was commonly performed as a dance for soloists at a burlesque comedy called a *jigg,* and several pieces called "jigs" were printed in early seventeenth-century collections of instrumental music.

By the 1650s, the jig was making the transition from popular entertainment to the realm of court musicians. The French lutenist Jacques Gautier was probably responsible for importing the dance from London, where he was a court musician for thirty years, to Paris. Shortly thereafter, French and German collections of dances for lute and for harpsichord began to include "gigues," which by then had come to refer to pieces featuring groupings of three or six beats.

Suites for keyboard instruments such as the harpsichord were particularly popular during the late seventeenth and early eighteenth centuries. Whether performed at Versailles for Louis XIV or in a more intimate *salon* in Paris or elsewhere in Europe, the dance suite normally consisted of at least four movements, sometimes introduced by a *prelude.* The conventional first movement was an *allemande,* a moderately quick dance in duple meter, originally of German origin. Next came a *courante,* a French dance performed at a moderate tempo that featured a rhythmic structure similar to that of the gigue. The third movement, a *sarabande,* was of Spanish origin and featured a slow triple meter. Finally, a *gigue* provided a lively way to close the suite. Other dances, such as the *bourrée, gavotte, minuet,* or *polonaise,* could be incorporated as well, either to supplement the standard movements or replace one or more of them. The general outline of this suite also held for orchestral suites, such as the *Water Music* and works to accompany ballets.

Recognized as a child prodigy, Elisabeth-Claude Jacquet de la Guerre (1665–1729) was given a musical education at the court at Versailles after Louis XIV heard her play the harpsichord. During the course of her thirty-two-year career, Jacquet de la Guerre wrote compositions for all three of the court's music departments, which provided chamber music, ceremonial and celebratory music, and church music. An active musician in the Parisian music scene, Jacquet de la Guerre established a *salon* in her home, that is, occasions for small audiences to enjoy a solo harpsichord performance, vocal music, or works for a chamber ensemble. Her Suite no. 1, published three years after she began giving harpsichord recitals in 1704, may be seen as part of a tradition established by French women who performed and patronized music in seventeenth-century France. Very likely, the composer performed this work as part of her recital series.

The first dance suite from Jacquet de la Guerre's *Pièces de clavecin qui peuvent se joüer sur le viollon (Pieces for Harpsichord That Can Be Played on the Violin)*, published in 1707, is somewhat longer than the traditional four-movement set. Three of the "extra" movements are *doubles,* in which the performer elaborates on the previous dance in an improvisatory style, and four others are tacked on at the end, after the usual gigue. The movements of this suite are as follows:

la flamande (an allemande) and double

courante and double

sarabande

gigue and double

second gigue

rigadoun (a dance in duple meter from the Provence region of France)

second rigadoun

chaconne (a composition in a slow triple meter built on a short repeating bass line)

The second gigue consists of two main sections, each of which is repeated. Each measure contains two groups of three beats counted as a fast ONE-two-three-FOUR-five-six, with accents falling on beats one and four. The rhythmic pattern "short-long, short-long" appears frequently, especially in the B section.

Near the end of the B section, a four-bar melody is played and then immediately repeated. The subtle change in volume and quality when the performer plays this repeated passage adds a new dimension to what would be an otherwise predictable repetition and is achieved by stepping on a pedal or manually activating a mechanism that changes the number of strings that are plucked when each key of the harpsichord is struck.

LISTEN TO the frequent ornaments, termed *mordents* or *trills,* that embellish the melodic line. Consider the radical transformation that the jig underwent to become a stylized, ornamented gigue. Note the occasional slowing down or speeding up of the music at important points in most performances of the work. Such expressive freedom, which was fine in a solo keyboard suite, would have created chaos if actual dancers had tried to coordinate with the music. The heavy ornamentation, too, obscures the regular meter and would make dancing to this piece awkward, to say the least. As the Baroque dance suite developed, both the sounds and meanings of the older dances were transformed by the new contexts in which these musics appeared.

CASE STUDY:

"Alla hornpipe" from *Water Music*

The hornpipe, like the jig, was imported from earlier times into new social and musical situations. The name hornpipe derives from the reed instrument with a cow horn at the end of its pipe that was used to accompany the dance four or more centuries ago. In the British Isles, the instrument has survived only in Wales, where it is called a *pibcorn,* but related instruments can still be found in Greece, North Africa, and Russia. The term *hornpipe* covers several different types of dances, including the solo dance, best known from its depiction on stage and in films, and a round dance, both usually in duple meter. By the eighteenth century, hornpipes were performed competitively at country gatherings, where increasingly complex dance steps were developed to exhibit a dancer's skill, emphasizing intricate footwork. Around the same time, the dance became associated with sailors across England; one writer reported in 1770 that "few English seamen are to be found that are not acquainted with it." Thanks in part to the widespread popularity of a single tune, with the title *The Sailors' Hornpipe* (although it has also been known as *The College Hornpipe*), the dance remains, to this day, associated with sailors.

In the late seventeenth century, a version of the hornpipe was created by dancing masters for more formal social occasions. This "refined" variant, which moves in triple meter at a moderate tempo, was borrowed by Handel to create a movement that incorporated one of the most popular and easily recognized themes of the early eighteenth century.

George Frideric Handel was born in Halle, Germany, in 1685. He was working as a keyboard player and composer when at age twenty-five, he was offered a position as chapel musician to the elector of Hanover. Handel accepted, but only on the condition that he could first spend a year in London. There he enjoyed a popular reception from Queen Anne and from the public. He returned to Hanover in 1711 only to travel once again to London in 1712. This time, however, Handel did not return to Germany within a "reasonable time" as promised; instead, he stayed in London, producing operas in Italian for the new opera house as well as ceremonial music and church music for Queen Anne. Her death in 1714 brought

Handel's former employer, the elector of Hanover, to London to assume the throne as King George I. According to a story first told in 1760, Handel was reinstated in the king's favor thanks to a clever plan conceived by a baron in the court who was an old friend of Handel's to surprise the king with Handel's music. On the evening of July 17, 1717, the king and his entourage set out on a barge and traveled up the Thames River to Chelsea. There, another barge, this one filled with musicians, provided some pre-supper entertainment. A Prussian resident of London, Friedrich Bonet, described the event two days later in a letter:

> Next to the King's barge was that of the musicians, about 50 in number, who played on all kinds of instruments, to wit trumpets, horns, hautboys [oboes], bassoons, German flutes, French flutes [probably recorders], violins and basses; but there were no singers. The music had been composed specially by the famous Handel, a native of Halle, and His Majesty's principal Court Composer. His Majesty approved of it so greatly that he caused it to be repeated three times in all, although each performance lasted an hour—namely twice before and once after supper. The [weather in the] evening was all that could be desired for the festivity, the number of barges and above all of boats filled with people desirous of hearing was beyond counting. . . . [The King] left at three o'clock and returned to St. James' about half past four.[1]

Although this wonderful story of Handel's reconciliation with his former employer is not wholly true—Handel was never entirely out of favor with the king—the barge performance must have been a magical event.

The *Water Music* consists of twenty-two dance pieces grouped into three separate suites in three different keys. Each suite highlights a specific orchestral instrument, the first emphasizing the French horns and the third featuring the flutes. In the second, which includes "Alla hornpipe," the trumpets are prominent. The seventeenth-century hornpipe is suggested by the moderately quick triple meter throughout the movement. Handel emphasizes the sounds of the brass, and avoids the lower registers of the strings and winds, which might be too soft to be heard outdoors. Even with these constraints, though, Handel was able to contrast the available instruments sharply, producing a back-and-forth dialogue.

The movement has two sections, with the marking *da capo* (Italian for "from the head") at the end of the **B** section, indicating that the entire **A** section is to be repeated exactly, thereby creating a three-part form. The **A** section begins with a melody stated by the strings and winds. This four-bar first theme may be thought of as a question that is immediately answered by the second theme (beginning with a high note repeated four times) in the same instruments. Next, two trumpets restate the first theme followed by two horns restating the theme yet again. The rest of the orchestra now plays the second theme, to be answered by the horns playing the second theme. Note how the same tune sounds different with each new orchestration. The dialogue continues; a third theme is introduced that is closely related to the second but with more sense of closure. This melody is passed from the orchestra to the trumpets to the horns, and back to the full orchestra as the **A** section comes to a close.

The **B** section begins with a short idea borrowed from the second theme of the **A** section. A somewhat polyphonic texture develops as the violins take the theme and run with it. Meanwhile, the other strings repeat one rhythmic idea over and over again—short-short-short-long, short-short-short-long—and the oboes softly weave a countermelody above the texture created by the other instruments. Eventually, the woodwinds drop out and allow the strings to bring the development section to a close.

LISTEN TO the hornpipe's main theme, which leads off the **A** section. Do you recognize it from its prominent use in an altogether different context? Think about the changing significance of this theme in different times, places, and contexts.

ADDITIONAL IMPORTANT TERMS

allemande	gigue	prelude
courante	harpsichord	salon
da capo	improvisation	sarabande
double	mordents	suite

CHAPTER

SEVEN

Music and Memory

Music and memory can interact in many ways: music can help us recall, reconstruct, and commemorate the past, and it can arouse thoughts and feelings that may reinforce and transform what we remember.

Almost any classical composition can illustrate how music both depends on memories and fosters new ones. Composers often use dedications to associate a work with the memory of a person, place, organization, or event. Sometimes, the text itself refers to memory: a famous example in Western music is the *aria* (solo song) from Henry Purcell's opera *Dido and Aeneas,* in which the dying Dido poignantly sings "remember me, but, ah, forget my fate." Song texts are most commonly used to embed information in our individual and collective memories and to cross the chasm of time between the past and the present. Many compositions, such as the Catholic Requiem Mass for the dead that originally shaped memory within a religious ceremony, also have a separate life in a concert setting, where their role in sustaining memory is muted though still very much present.

Two examples illustrate different ways in which music and memory interact. If we examine J. S. Bach's Cantata no. 80, *Ein feste Burg ist unser Gott* ("A Mighty Fortress Is Our God"), we will see how a melody can hold special significance for the collective memory of a congregation while also giving shape to a musical form. The second example, Beethoven's *Symphony No. 5,* imprints its short and distinctive musical theme into the memory of the listener. So indelible has this theme proven to be that it has been continually remembered—and re-interpreted—over the course of two centuries.

44

CASE STUDY:

Bach's *A Mighty Fortress Is Our God* (cantata)

Although Johann Sebastian Bach (1685–1750) produced a great quantity of instrumental music, including many works that have become part of the standard repertoire, it is his vocal music that concerns us here. As music director at several churches and cantor of the St. Thomas Church in Leipzig from 1723 until his death, one of Bach's chief responsibilities was to perform a *cantata*—a narrative musical work for soloists, choir (usually), and orchestra—for every Sunday of the church calendar. Cantatas were a prominent part of the Lutheran worship service. Their texts, related generally to the Gospel reading for the day, could be taken from a variety of sources, including the Bible, hymnals, or newly written poetry. Between 1723 and 1729, Bach composed four complete annual cycles of sixty cantatas, from which around two hundred cantatas survive.

Bach's sacred cantatas typically contain between five and eight movements. Typically, the first and final movements (and sometimes one or more others) call for a choir, while the other sections are performed by one or several solo singers. The solo arias resemble opera arias of the day, consisting of formal songs introduced by speechlike declamation, called *recitative*. A full orchestra, including flutes, oboes, bassoons, trumpets, timpani, strings, and organ, was available to fill out the sound.

Most often, a cantata was based on a *chorale*, or hymn tune, that was known and loved by the congregation. Chorales, which held a special significance for Lutherans because they symbolized the solidarity of the congregation in its worship of God, were introduced to the German Protestant church service by Martin Luther in the early sixteenth century. For the congregants, the chorales were closely connected to memory: singing chorales reminded them of Martin Luther, the great Reformer of their church; commemorated important figures and events from the Bible while linking them with contemporary times; and welded the congregants, who joined the choir in singing, into a powerful whole, reminding them of their common beliefs and shared—often transcendent—religious experiences.

In many cantatas of Bach's time, the Lutheran chorale serves yet another function related to memory: the chorale tune appears in the first and last movements, at least, reminding congregants of earlier movements when they reach the end of the work. In the final movement, the full choir sings the chorale in a traditional, homophonic arrangement, with the congregation presumably joining in. Hearing the chorale embedded in the musical fabric of the cantata and finally singing the simple, unpretentious, and unaltered chorale together helped the community form a collective congregational memory.

The cantata *A Mighty Fortress Is Our God* is based on a chorale composed by Martin Luther in 1529. This hymn, which draws on the text of Psalm 46, was a popular musical symbol of all the church reforms that Luther initiated. Bach set the first verse of the chorale in the first movement, the second verse in the second movement, the third verse in the fifth movement, and the fourth verse in the eighth movement. The libretto for the remaining movements, by the poet Salomo Franck, is based on the Gospel according to St. Luke (11:14–28). This passage, which describes Jesus' exorcism of the devil from a man, shares with the chorale text the theme that God is the ultimate source of strength in the battle against evil. Bach first composed the cantata in a shorter version in 1715, well before he moved to the St. Thomas School. At Leipzig, he revised his original setting, adding the opening chorus and one other movement, for use at a 1730 festival. The cantata was revised several times more during Bach's life, suggesting that it must have been performed with some frequency. The version generally performed today is a synthesis of these later versions.

The eight movements of the revised form of the cantata are symmetrical, with choral movements at the ends and in the middle, duets for movements two and seven, and solo movements in between:

1. Chorale (chorus, fugal setting)
2. Duet (soprano/bass)
3. Recitativo and arioso (bass solo)
4. Aria (soprano solo)
5. Chorale (unison chorus, polyphonic setting)
6. Recitativo (tenor solo)
7. Duet (alto/tenor)
8. Chorale (chorus, homophonic setting)

LISTEN TO the last movement first to become familiar with the chorale in its most straightforward form. The text is set in four-part harmony with a homophonic texture. The simplicity of the melody, clearly audible in the soprano part, has prompted comparisons to German "folk" tunes, which always figured prominently both in Lutheran ideology and in German writings about identity. Try listening a few times to the chorale, humming along, and learning the melody. The melody of lines one and two is repeated for lines three and four, making this tune easier to remember. Also note the slight asymmetry in the two stanzas: the first stanza consists of four lines, and the second stanza has one line appended, almost like a *coda*.

8. CHORALE

Das Wort sie sollen lassen stahn	Now let the Word of God abide
und kein Dank dazu haben.	without further thought.
Er ist bei uns wohl auf dem Plan	He is firmly on our side
mit seinem Geist und Gaben.	with His spirit and strength.
Nehmen sie uns dein Leib,	Though they deprive us of life,
Gut Ehr', Kind, und Weib,	wealth, honor, child, and wife,
lass fahren dahin,	we will not complain,
sie haben's kein Gewinn;	it will avail them nothing;
das Reich muss uns doch bleiben.	for God's kingdom must prevail.

Turn now to the opening movement of the cantata, which uses the text from the first verse of Luther's chorale.

1. CHORUS

Ein feste Burg ist unser Gott,	A mighty fortress is our God,
ein' gute Wehr und Waffen;	a good defense and weapon;
er hilft uns frei aus aller Not,	He helps free us from all the troubles
die uns jetzt hat betroffen.	that have now befallen us.
Der alte böse Feind,	Our ever-evil foe,
mit Ernst er's jetzt meint,	in earnest plots against us,
gross Macht und viel List	with great strength and cunning
sein grausam Rüstung ist;	he prepares his dreadful plans.
auf Erd' ist nicht seinsgleichen.	Earth holds none like him.

Now listen to the first movement. The tenors begin the fugue by singing an elaborate version of the chorale melody. As the tenors come to the end of the first line, the altos enter singing the same melody, but at the interval of a fifth above the tenors. Next the sopranos enter and finally the basses, each presenting the same melody but starting it on a different pitch. Each voice is *doubled* by a section of the string instruments—that is, the first violins play with the sopranos, the second violins with the altos, and so forth—to further enrich the sound.

LISTEN FOR the entry of the trumpet, high up in its range, playing the simple chorale melody, followed by the string basses, playing the chorale melody in a very low register; the trumpet provides an echo of the chorale melody throughout the first movement. As the movement continues, voices come in and drop out, and the texture alternately thins and thickens, but the chorale melody welds the course of events into a unified whole. By the time the movement is ended, the short and simple melody of the chorale *Ein feste Burg ist unser Gott* has been heard repeatedly, so Bach's listeners could not help but remember the Lutheran melody and all that it represented.

CASE STUDY:

Beethoven's Symphony no. 5

Over the years, the composer Ludwig van Beethoven (1770–1827) has been portrayed as the consummate artist-genius: his fiery personality, unkempt looks, and innovative music have fused into a distinctive popular image. The view of Beethoven as the quintessential Romantic artist-genius began during his own lifetime and still influences the way listeners continue to hear and interpret his music. Beethoven's *Fifth Symphony* has one of the most memorable themes in the classical repertoire, a characteristic that has insured both its continued transmission and its many reinterpretations over time.

Beethoven composed the Fifth Symphony mostly between 1804 and 1808, the year of its premiere. The central musical idea of the work is announced immediately: a four-note motive (musical theme) set to a rhythm of three short beats followed by a long beat. Beethoven uses this motive throughout the entire symphony to unify the work. The first movement develops the motive within a fairly conventional *sonata-form* structure (a form we first encountered in Piazzolla's *Adios Nonino* in chapter 6). In the first major section of this form, the *exposition,* the memorable four-note theme is presented in the key of C minor and a songlike second theme in the woodwinds enters for contrast in E♭ major. After the exposition section is repeated, we hear a *development* section, in which the four-note main theme is repeated and varied. Then in the *recapitulation,* the first and second themes return, both in C minor, with a *coda* bringing the movement to a close.

After its premiere on December 2, 1808, in Vienna, Beethoven's Fifth was recognized immediately as a "great symphony," as one reviewer wrote then. Following the first performance outside Germany—in England in 1829—the symphony's reputation had grown so strong that the Philharmonic Society of New York programmed it to lead off its first-ever public concert in 1842. The composer Schumann wrote of Beethoven's Fifth Symphony: "Every time it is performed it exercises an unvarying power on us, like natural phenomena which fill us with awe and amazement every time they occur."

This symphony, and especially its main theme, have taken on different meanings for different people. Many have associated the symphony's motive with the idea of fate as expressed in Beethoven's writings. Around the time that he made the first preliminary sketches for the Fifth Symphony in 1801, Beethoven remarked to a friend that "I will take Fate by the throat, it will not wholly overcome me."

In twentieth-century Russia, both Lenin and Stalin seized on the humanist qualities that have been associated with this and other Beethoven symphonies and hailed it as the "anthem of human freedom." Also during this period, Adolf Hitler claimed Beethoven's compositions as part of the German cultural heritage inherited by the Third Reich. In an ironic twist, the famous motive from the Fifth Symphony was also appropriated by the British Broadcasting Company during World War II. The rhythmic pattern "short-short-short-long" corresponds to the Morse code symbol for the letter V, so every BBC broadcast began with a quotation of this musical idea to signal "V for Victory." Memories of Beethoven, and in particular the meaning of his Fifth Symphony's main motive, have been repeatedly recalled and transformed for political purposes of many types.

One need only listen to the other three movements of the Fifth Symphony to hear yet more appearances of the main motive. The second movement of the symphony features a *theme-and-variations* form, during which the short-short-short-long rhythmic pattern appears many times. It can be heard at the end of the presentation of the first theme—first in the violins, then in the flutes, then in the violins again. The second theme, presented immediately thereafter by the clarinets, is also based on an extended short-short-short-long pattern.

The third movement, with its *scherzo* form (a quick and playful movement taking its name from the Italian word for 'joke') also incorporates the rhythm of the main motive. After the basses and cellos present two melodies at the beginning of the movement, the horns begin playing an insistent short-short-short-long pattern that is heard almost constantly throughout the first and final sections of the scherzo. It has been suggested that the contrast between the deep, dark melody of the basses and the militant blasts of the horns represents a mental conflict, a struggle against fate.

The fourth movement, like the first movement, is in *sonata form*. The movement is in the key of C major, and the shift from the prevailing minor mode of the other movements to the major mode has been said to represent the triumph of the individual over fate, of the "human" over "destiny." Once again, the short-short-short-long pattern appears prominently in the rhythm of the second theme and the supposed "victory" over fate is proclaimed decisively and triumphantly in the finale.

(For further analysis and a more detailed walk-through, see the multimedia "Enhanced Listening Guide" on *The Norton Recordings, Shorter Version* CD-ROM.)

LISTEN FOR the many appearances of the main motive throughout the four movements of the entire symphony.

ADDITIONAL IMPORTANT TERMS

aria	exposition	Requiem Mass
cantata	motive	scherzo
chorale	recapitulation	sonata form
development	recitative	

CHAPTER

EIGHT

Music and Identity

Identity can be expressed through musical creativity and performance. We can see personal identities expressed through a flute concerto and karaoke, and collective ethnic affiliations symbolized by Cajun and Zydeco songs. Here, we explore two instances in which music and identity are closely linked. We turn first to an orchestral work by the nineteenth-century Czech composer Bedřich Smetana in which national identity is asserted through music during a time of political and social upheaval in Bohemia. Then, we explore George Bizet's opera *Carmen* and see how a popular late-nineteenth-century composition characterized identity related to gender roles.

CASE STUDY:

The Moldau from My Fatherland

In 1824, the year Bedřich Smetana was born, musical composition in Czech-speaking Bohemia was in a confused state. On the one hand, the cult of Mozart and the classical Austro-Germanic tradition dominated in major cities like Prague. On the other hand, the relatively enlightened policies of the Hapsburg Emperor Josef II had given Bohemians just enough freedom to allow a revival of Czech literature and history, which would lead the way to the Czech nationalist movement. Czech art music lagged behind this rebirth of Czech culture; only in 1826 was the first Czech-language opera composed.

By 1846, Smetana had left his small native town of Litomysl for Prague, birth-place of the Czech Nationalist movement, where he struggled as a pianist, music teacher, and budding composer. Political instability forced Emperor Ferdinand, Josef's successor, to abdicate in March 1848, allowing the young Czech political movement to stage an uprising. By summer, though, the rebels had been defeated and the Austrian government cracked down on the movement with a harsh wave of reprisals, censorship, and travel restrictions that effectively isolated Bohemia for a decade from the world beyond the borders of the Empire.

The level of Smetana's involvement in the Revolution of 1848 is unclear. He was certainly a member of the citizen's army called *Svornost* ("United"), where he met one of the leaders of the Czech movement, Karel Sabina, who would later write the libretti for Smetana's first operas. Inspired by the movement, some of Smetana's earliest compositions were patriotic works such as *Two Marches* for mil-itary band or piano. We must ask ourselves why these works quote the Hapsburg Imperial Anthem (originally a tune by the composer Joseph Haydn) and a German student song. This seeming paradox may be resolved when we understand that although Smetana yearned for the Czech people's freedom, he also hoped for a reconciliation with Austria by which Bohemia would obtain some autonomy with-out breaking away from the Empire. Smetana's songs for the revolution are more clearly patriotic; his *Song of Freedom,* for example, was intended to be the anthem of the citizen's army, *Svornost.* Jan Žižka mentioned in the text, is a Bohemian war hero of the early fifteenth century; Tábor is a city he founded.

> War! War! does the flag fly?
> Rise up ye Czechs, for God is with us!
> Stand firmly for your rights.
> Guard your country and the glory of the Czechs!
> The clamour that fills the air is
> The sound of Žižka and of Tábor![1]

Thus began Smetana's quest to found—or invent—a new Czech musical tra-dition. Smetana composed several operas in the 1860s, a period in which the Czech Nationalist movement experienced a resurgence. Although several of these works were successful, his 1868 opera *Dalibor* was criticized for being too "German" by conservative Czech Nationalists, who firmly believed that Czech music should be modeled on traditional folk tunes. In 1874, Smetana rapidly lost his hearing but, like Beethoven, clung to composing despite the hardship and began writing a cycle of *symphonic poems* (single movement works for orchestra that followed a program) called *Má Vlast* (*My Fatherland*). Four of its movements were done by October 1875, and the whole work was completed in March 1879.

The six programmatic movements of *Má Vlast* literally map Smetana's country, with musical representations of geographic features such as mountains, rivers, valleys, fields, and forests, as well as the town Tábor, which symbolized the national revolutionary spirit.

In the second movement, Smetana traced the course of the river Vltava, or Moldau. Beginning in the Sumava Mountains, the Moldau flows through Bohemia and Prague until it merges with the Elbe. The musical composition roughly parallels this course, as Smetana makes clear in May 1879 in a letter to his publisher:

> The composition depicts the course of the river, from its beginning where two brooks, one cold, the other warm, join a stream, running through forests and meadows and a lovely countryside where merry feasts are celebrated; water-sprites dance in the moonlight; on nearby rocks can be seen the outline of ruined castles, proudly soaring into the sky. Vltava swirls through the St. John Rapids and flows in a broad stream towards Prague. It passes Vyšehrad and disappears majestically into the distance, where it joins the Elbe.[2]

The inspiration for this work came during an 1867 trip taken by Smetana with two friends in the countryside of the Sumava Valley. According to one of his companions, Smetana stood at the meeting point of the warm and cold streams, the Otava and the Vydra, and contemplated the starting point of the Moldau.

My Fatherland was very warmly received at its premiere in 1882; without doubt, the combination of Czech myth, history, and scenic imagery contributed to the work's popularity. Smetana's friends and admirers soon suggested cycles based on other historical figures and characters from Czech myths, but the composer declined to follow up on these ideas. *My Fatherland* remains Smetana's most fervent expression of nationalism and one of the masterpieces of national music.

The musical form of *The Moldau* follows the program laid out by the composer. The movement begins by evoking the running water of the river's source. A single flute, representing the small brook at the source of the river, begins playing a gurgling melody. It is soon joined by a second flute, as the intensity slowly starts to build. A pair of clarinets enters, and eventually the violas contribute to the thickening texture. As the woodwinds drop out, the lower strings pick up the sound of rushing water and the first violins (along with some of the woodwinds) play the main *Moldau* theme, a sweeping melody in the key of E minor. After the

second statement, the composer modulates to E major and the theme is presented in major mode. The theme is slightly expanded, then repeated.

The second section of *The Moldau* depicts a hunting scene as the river flows
through a forest; the horns announce this passage with a *fanfare*. All along, the
rushing water continues in the strings, even during this forest scene. As the
horns fade into the distance, we come upon a rustic village wedding. We hear
the dance tune changing in intensity and orchestration to enliven the music.
When the wedding scene fades out, woodwinds creep in to evoke the river in
the moonlight. Flutes, punctuated occasionally by the harp, suggest the dance
of water nymphs.

When the dance ends, the broad *Moldau* theme returns in its original minor key
as the rushing water theme becomes intense in the lower strings. The rapids eventually calm down and slow to a trickle; suddenly, the Moldau turns a corner and
the rich, wide river can be seen in all its glory. The Vltava melody is triumphantly
played in a major key by the entire orchestra. As it proceeds, the river flows by the
Vyšehrad hill; all the instruments except the strings play the Vyšehrad motive from
the first movement of the cycle. The piece ebbs and flows on the way to an
emphatic cadence.

The *Moldau* theme is today sung as a folk tune throughout the Czech Republic,
with a simple rhyming text that translates as "The cat crawls through the hole, and
the dog through the window." Indeed, this melody has folklike qualities and may
have been borrowed directly from a Czech traditional tune that was little known
by mid-nineteenth-century Czechs. It does, however, bear a striking resemblance
to a Swedish melody popular at the time, *Ach, Beautiful Vermland.* Smetana had
in fact spent five years living in Sweden, from 1856 to 1861. Very likely, this
Swedish folk tune, popularized in a hit 1846 play, *The Vermland People,* was appropriated by Smetana and only later became a popular Czech folk tune. This fine
example of musical migration and borrowing shows, specifically, how identity can
be invented and evoked through music.

LISTEN TO the detailed representation of the river and the lands through which
it flows. For example, note how the intensity builds when the listener arrives at the
St. John's Rapids. What do you think Smetana intends to represent at this point
through the contrasting rhythms in the horns and trumpets, and in the flutes and
piccolos?

CASE STUDY:

The Habañera from *Carmen*

Dramatic musical genres such as opera, and the identities of their characters, reflect the attitudes, mores, and prejudices of a culture. Here we will discuss an excerpt from the opera *Carmen,* by the Parisian Georges Bizet. The work, written for a Paris audience, was premiered on March 3, 1875, at the Opéra-Comique, one of the two major French opera houses of its day. It aimed to attract a broad, non-elite audience that was accustomed to the use of spoken dialogue in music dramas.

Bizet composed *Carmen* near the end of his short career, which was marred after a promising start by failed works and chronic illness. He chose a *libretto* (text of the opera) that was based on Prosper Mérimée's short novel of the same title. Bizet was attracted by the story's setting in Spain, which was viewed by the late-nineteenth-century French as sharing "exotic" qualities of mystery and barbarism with the Middle East and beyond. Its main character, Carmen, is a *femme fatale* who preys on a male victim, Don José. The opera was not well received initially; its plot and music were criticized in Paris as being obscene and repulsive. However, after a Vienna performance in October 1875, *Carmen* soon achieved international popularity, which continues to this day.

On the surface, *Carmen* is the story of an ill-fated love affair between a seductive Spanish Romani (Gypsy) woman and an innocent male soldier. The action is set in Seville, the first scene taking place outside the cigarette factory where Carmen works and near the army barracks where José is quartered. Carmen is arrested for fighting in the factory but gains her freedom by seducing her guard, José, who is then clapped in jail himself for allowing her to escape. In act 2, after his release, José joins Carmen at an inn. But then, instead of returning to his barracks, he follows Carmen to the mountains. Act 3 finds the couple at a smuggler's headquarters in the mountains, with José consumed by guilt over having deserted both the army and his fiancée, Micaela, who arrives to tell José that his mother is ill. Carmen meanwhile shifts her affection to the bullfighter Escamillo. Before heading back to Seville, the jealous José quarrels with his rival and threatens Carmen as he departs. In act 4, Carmen is back in Seville, on her way to a bullfight with her new lover Escamillo. She pauses to talk with José, who intercepts her in the square. After Carmen refuses his entreaties to return to him, José stabs her to death as the sounds of the bullfight are heard in the background.

Despite its conventional dramatic characters and its plot featuring jealousy and tragic love, *Carmen* can be seen to embody and convey a number of widespread beliefs in nineteenth-century Paris about race, class, and gender. Composed during a period in which the French and other Europeans were fascinated with the foreign cultures they had begun to conquer and colonize, the opera held multiple layers of signification for its French audiences. Just as Spain represented the Orient, with which it was linked in the French imagination, Don José stood for the everyday man who encounters and is subsequently undone by an exotic "other"— in this case, a Romani temptress. The French tended to classify Roma (Gypsies) as Orientals, all of whom they regarded with suspicion as both dangerous and treacherous.

In addition to exploiting period stereotypes of race and ethnicity, the opera raises issues of class and sexuality. Carmen is a dishonest employee of a cigarette factory who fights with her co-workers. These aspects of Carmen's character reflect the tensions between the middle class and working class that permeated France during the mid-nineteenth century and resurfaced as late as 1871, just four years before the opera was premiered.[3]

Finally, the portrayals of Carmen and Micaela, the other major female character, present two opposite views of women that were widely accepted in nineteenth-century Paris—often by the same individual. This familiar cultural ambivalence shows up in the characters of the two women. Micaela is the stereotypically passive, selfless woman who puts the man's welfare before her own, while Carmen is the dangerous, sexually assertive woman who threatens men. The real-life model for Carmen may have been Céleste Vénard, a famous French courtesan, singer, and writer in Paris whom Bizet knew well.

All the aspects of identity portrayed in the plot—race, ethnicity, class, and gender—resonate with attitudes held in Parisian culture at the time. It is clear, then, that the social setting of *Carmen* contributed to both its content and its significance. If we turn to the *Habañera,* a famous *aria* (solo song) from the opera, we can better understand how musical sound itself was used to underscore and convey these different identities.

Carmen was composed as an *opéra comique,* a type of opera distinguished by having dialogue that is spoken rather than sung. (Shortly after Bizet's death, another composer set *Carmen's* spoken dialogue to music; this revised version of the opera is the one most often heard in opera houses today.) However, *Carmen* differs from other operas of the type in that its story has neither the usual sentimental plot nor the usual happy ending. Some of its most striking musical characteristics result from the composer's specific efforts to convey the exoticism of the opera's setting and characters through its music. Bizet did some exploration and actually drew on music by Spanish composers at two points in the opera, most notably for the *Habañera,* which derived its music from *El Arreglito,* a song by the Spanish composer Sebastián Yradier.

Bizet may have heard *El Arreglito* from Vénard, who performed at a popular Paris cafe. Yradier himself, a Spanish voice teacher who lived in Paris, borrowed the melody for the song from Afro-Cuban music he heard during his travels to the Caribbean and South America. Thus we end up with the curious situation that the *habañera* rhythm, from which Bizet's aria takes its title, is invoked to represent an imagined Spain but is known to have originated in Cuba.

The *Habañera* provides a fine instance in which a melody is transmitted and transformed, starting as the tune for a Caribbean folksong, then moving to a Parisian cabaret song, and finally finding its way into an opera aria. It typifies how the "exotic" was portrayed in European music of its time. Bizet's setting of the song, with its habañera rhythms, underscores Carmen's seductive walk and hip motions and emphasizes Carmen's open sensuality and female sexuality. Additionally, the descending *chromatic* melody—a melody that descends by half-steps, the smallest interval in the Western musical system—was a musical gesture that was used, along with pentatonic scales, by Bizet and other European composers of the period to convey a sense of the exotic, the primitive, and the alien. Describing these purported "Spanish" or "Oriental" gestures simply as examples of exoticism in Western music sidesteps the Europeans' ideological view of Orientalism as being closely related to misogyny. And the musical fabric of Carmen is steeped in both of these.

LISTEN TO the *Habañera* from act 1 of *Carmen,* following both the *habañera* rhythm and the descending, chromatic melody used to convey multiple aspects of identity. Note, too, that the text of the song underscores aspects of identity conveyed in the music.

CARMEN

L'amour est un oiseau rebelle	Love is a rebellious bird
que nul ne peut apprivoiser,	that nobody can tame,
et c'est bien en vain qu'on l'appelle	and it's simply no good calling it
s'il lui convient de refuser.	if it suits it to refuse;
Rien n'y fait, menace ou prière,	neither threat nor prayer will prevail.
l'un parle bien, l'autre se tait;	One of them talks, the other holds his peace.
et c'est l'autre que je préfère;	and I prefer the other one!
il n'a rien dit, mais il me plaît.	He hasn't said a word, but I like him!

CHORUS

L'amour est un oiseau . . .   Love is a rebellious bird . . .

CARMEN

L'amour! L'amour! L'amour!   Love! Love! Love!
L'amour est enfant de Bohème,   Love is a Gypsy,
il n'a jamais connu de loi,   it has never been subject to any law.
si tu m'aimes pas, je t'aime;   If you do not love me, I love you;
si je t'aime, prends garde à toi!   if I love you, take care!

CHORUS

Prends garde à toi!. . .   Take care! . . .

CARMEN

L'oiseau que tu croyais surprendre   The bird you thought to surprise
battit de l'aile et s'envola;   has spread its wings and flown;
l'amour est loin, tu peux l'attendre;   love is far away, you may wait for it;
tu ne l'attends plus, il est là!   when you've given up waiting, it is there!
Tout autour de toi vite, vite,   All around you, quickly, quickly
il vient, s'en va, puis il revient;   it comes, goes, and comes again.
Tu crois le tenir, il t'évite;   You think you've caught it, it escapes you;
Tu crois l'éviter, il te tient!   you think to escape it, you are caught!

CHORUS

Tout autour de toi . . .   All around you . . .

CARMEN

L'amour! L'amour! . . .   Love! Love! . . .

CHORUS OF GIRLS

L'amour est enfant de Bohème . . .   Love is a Gypsy . . .

ADDITIONAL IMPORTANT TERMS

chromatic	*opéra comique*
habañera	symphonic poem
libretto	

CHAPTER

NINE NINE NINE NINE NINE NINE NINE NINE NINE NINE NINE NINE NINE NINE NINE NINE NINE NINE NINE NINE NINE NINE NINE

Music and Politics

National anthems can proclaim "official" political ideologies celebrating the traditions, beliefs, and propaganda of those in power. But the same ideologies can also be used subversively, as music becomes a rallying cry or a weapon of empowerment for weaker or oppressed groups. One example, *Nkosi Sikelele iAfrika*, encompassed both of these roles, starting as a song of resistance and becoming a national anthem as the political situation in South Africa changed momentously in the 1990s.

As we might expect, music and politics influence one another just as much in Western classical soundscapes. The reinforcement of Czech national identity through Smetana's *My Fatherland* certainly had political motivations and implications. Between the sixteenth and nineteenth centuries wealthy and powerful patrons provided the primary means of support for many composers and could commission music for political ends. Consider Handel's *Water Music*, written for an elaborate festive occasion shortly after the ascension of King George to the throne; certainly, without such music and such parties, the King's stature and prominence in the public eye would have been considerably diminished. The use of Beethoven's music as a symbol in both British and German propaganda during World War II is yet another example.

CASE STUDY:
Alexander Nevsky

A work by the Russian composer Sergei Prokofiev embodies an official ideology with a utilitarian intent. Prokofiev composed *Alexander Nevsky* in 1938, when the renowned film director Sergei Eisenstein was asked to create a nationalistic work to bolster Russian morale in the face of a threat from the Nazi government in Germany. Since this was to be Eisenstein's first film with sound, it was a great honor for Prokofiev to be chosen to compose the score. The resulting collaboration redefined how music and film could interact. The movie was a success, and the score was later revised as a *cantata* (in this case, a secular multimovement work for voice and orchestra) that was premiered in April 1942, shortly before the German invasion had its deepest penetration into the Soviet Union and even Moscow seemed in danger of capture. But the *Alexander Nevsky* music cannot be described simply as a work of wartime propaganda. Despite Prokofiev's obvious reluctance to involve himself with politics, his artistic choices were, in fact, shaped by the startling shifts in the Russian political, social, and aesthetic landscapes that occurred during his lifetime.

Sergei Prokofiev (1891–1953) was born in a small Ukrainian town during the rule of Tsar Alexander III. His family was reasonably well-off, and throughout his youth he was encouraged to pursue his academic and musical studies at the St. Petersburg Conservatory rather than focus on the political world around him. Nevertheless, the shocking events of Bloody Sunday, when hundreds of unarmed protesters were shot by the Tsar's troops in January 1905, must have made an impression. This massacre started a chain of events that ultimately led to the Russian Revolution of 1917. As the Bolsheviks began to gain control in 1918 and the Russian economy fell apart, Prokofiev left St. Petersburg for New York.

Prokofiev soon moved to Paris, where he enjoyed a successful career as a pianist and composer. When he returned to Russia in 1929, Joseph Stalin had taken firm control of the Soviet Union and his government actively censored works of literature, music, theater, and art that were considered too leftist (avant-garde) or too rightist ("bourgeois intellectual"). All artistic creations were supposed to exhibit "Socialist realism," a vague term invented by Stalin in 1932 to encourage works that would appeal to the proletariat—the working classes— rather than to the intellectual elite. When Prokofiev found himself being interrogated by Communist Party officials about his music, he replied, "That concerns politics, not music, and therefore I won't answer." Despite his antipolitical attitudes, however, Prokofiev was forced to modify his compositional goals and methods to meet the demands of the Soviet government.

The film director Sergei Eisenstein (1898–1948) narrowly escaped official condemnation himself when he first agreed to create a film about Alexander Nevsky, a thirteenth-century Russian military hero who took his name from the Neva River, where he defeated the German army in 1240. The movie dealt with the most famous battle of Nevsky's career, a decisive victory over German forces on the frozen Lake Chudskoe on April 5, 1242. The film was produced on a very tight schedule—in only five months—and yet Eisenstein and Prokofiev achieved an unprecedented interdependence of musical and visual imagery.

Prokofiev decided to use melodies that sounded like Russian folk tunes but avoided borrowing actual melodies. As he explained,

> The action of the film takes place in the thirteenth century and is built up on two opposing elements: the Russians on the one hand, and the Teutonic knights on the other. The temptation to make use of the actual music of the period was naturally great. But a brief acquaintance with Catholic thirteenth-century choral singing was enough to show that this music has in the past seven centuries become far too remote and emotionally alien to us . . . to stimulate the imagination of the present-day film spectator. We therefore decided not to reproduce it as it sounded at the time of the Battle on the Ice seven centuries ago but to adapt it to the modern ear. The same applies to the Russian music of the period; that too had to be given a modern ring.[1]

The seventh and final movement of the cantata depicts "Alexander's Entry into Pskov," as the Russian army returns triumphantly home after defeating the German forces. This movement begins with a homophonic choral section, the "Chorus of Russians," singing a patriotic text with a full orchestral accompaniment, including prominent brass and percussion.

A quicker, lighter section follows, with bells, xylophone, and pizzicato strings evoking a joyous dance tune as the women sing a celebratory melody. The men's voices then reenter, responding to the women by imitating their melody. Men and women combine to sing the "Motherland Russia" theme, recalling a melody presented earlier, in the fourth movement.

Next we hear an orchestral passage that features a motive introduced by the trumpets and flutes and then imitated by other instruments. The motive is sometimes inverted—turned upside down—so that the quick upward gesture becomes a quick downward gesture. The woodwinds are emphasized. Then, the "Motherland Russia" theme is presented in several different renditions by the choir. The brass and percussion can be heard prominently as the finale comes to a close.

Even before the film was completely edited, Stalin sent a message in the middle of the night, demanding to see the film. In their nervous haste, the production staff failed to include one reel of film, which was to be edited the next day. The film gained the approval of Stalin, but the director decided to discard the ten minutes of film he had failed to send rather than risk invoking the dictator's wrath by including it. Creating *Alexander Nevsky* required conforming to the ideology of the Soviet state. Despite Prokofiev's apolitical aesthetic ideals, it became clear that he would not be allowed to continue composing if he failed to adapt his music to a style conforming to Stalin's ideology.

When the soundtrack was originally recorded for the film, Prokofiev discovered, quite by accident, that musicians placed too close to a microphone could produce a sound that overpowered the rest of the orchestra. He decided to use this effect to his advantage, controlling the musicians' distances from the microphone in order to make a trombone or a trumpet sound small or weak and a bassoon sound formidable. In another film-music first, chorus and orchestra were recorded separately and then spliced together so that their relative volume levels could be balanced more accurately.

LISTEN without benefit of the visual images and consider how the impact of the cantata might vary from that of the film score in its cinematic setting.

CHORUS OF RUSSIANS

Na vyliki boi vykhodila Rus'.	Russia marched out to mighty battle.
Voroga pobyedila Rus'.	Russia overcame the enemy.
Na rodnoi zyemlye nye byvat' vragu.	On our native soil, let no foe exist.
Kto pridyot, budyet nasmyert' bit.	Whoever invades will be killed.

WOMEN

Vyesyelisya, poi, mat'rodnaya Rus'!	Be merry, sing, mother Russia!
Na rodnoi Rusi nye byvat' vragu.	In our native Russia, let no foe exist.
Kto pridyol na Rus', budyet nasmert' bit.	Let no foe see our native villages.
Nye' vidat' vragu nashikh russikh syol.	Whoever invades Russia will be killed.

MEN

Nye vidat' vragu nashikh, russikh syol.	Let no foe see our native villages.
Kto pridyot na Rus', budyet nasmert' bit.	Whoever invades Russia will be killed.

CHORUS OF RUSSIANS

Na Rusi rodnoi, na Rusi bol'shoi nye byvat' vragu.	In our native Russia, in great Russia, let no foe exist.
Na Rusi rodnoi, na Rusi bol'shoi nye byat' vragu.	In our native Russia, in great Russia, let no foe exist.
Vyesyelisya, poi, mat' rodnaya Rus'!	Be merry, sing, mother Russia!
Na vyelikii prazdnik sobralasya Rus'.	At the mighty festival, all Russia has gathered together.
Vyesyelisya, Rus'! rodnaya mat'!	Be merry, Russia, mother of ours!

CASE STUDY:

Vocalise for the Angel Who Announces the End of Time from *Quartet for the End of Time*

Where *Alexander Nevsky* expressed an official ideology, the *Quartet for the End of Time* by Olivier Messiaen (1908–1992) is a piece of resistance, written during 1941 in desperate circumstances: the composer was a prisoner in Stalag VIII, a Nazi work camp. Messiaen had been an up-and-coming French composer in 1930s Paris. In his early works, he explored unconventional musical scales and meters, such as the compound metric patterns of Greek song and classical Indian rhythms. From his study of ancient Indian music, Messiaen borrowed complex *palindromic* rhythmic patterns—that is, they sound the same when played forward or backward.

In World War II, Messiaen enlisted as an assistant in the French medical corps and was captured by the Germans in June 1940 near the city of Nancy. The composer, carrying little more than some miniature musical scores that he happened to have with him (including music by Bach, Beethoven, Ravel, Stravinsky, and Berg), was sent by rail to Görlitz, a small town fifty-five miles from Dresden in southeastern Germany. But Messiaen's painful experience was not completely without hope, for his German captors allowed him to keep his scores and provided him with music paper, pencils, and erasers. Among his fellow prisoners were a cellist, a clarinetist, and a violinist, who managed to find serviceable instruments. The German officers allowed the ensemble to rehearse each evening at 6 o'clock, Messiaen wrote the quartet for this group and played the piano part himself on a broken-down, out-of-tune upright piano. The piece was performed on January 15, 1941, in a large unheated hut, before an audience of five thousand prisoners.

The indelible nature of this experience and of the music at its center was under-scored forty years later. In the autumn of 1981, the British musician Charles Bodman Rae visited Poland and stayed with the Polish architect Aleksander Lyczewski in his Warsaw apartment. Rae was practicing for an upcoming per-formance of the *Quartet* (*Quatuor* in French). Rae later wrote what happened as he practiced the piece in Lyczewski's apartment:

> I heard Aleksander Lyczewski rushing downstairs from his painting studio and he then burst into my room with a mixed expression of confusion and distress on his face. He said he recognised the piece I was playing and wanted to know who had composed it. He sat down and I explained about Messiaen and the circumstances under which the **Quatuor** had been written and first performed. He then recounted to me his experience as a prisoner of war in the same camp at Görlitz in Silesia. Aleksander was in a very emotional state while he was recalling these events. There were tears in his eyes and it took some time for him to regain his composure. He had been present at the first performance and vividly recalled the atmosphere in the large freezing hut where hundreds of prisoners (many Poles, other central Europeans, and some French) assembled to hear the piece. Apparently there were even wounded prisoners, brought from the hospital block, lying on stretchers at the front of the audience. He remembers his fellow-prisoners remaining in complete silence for the hour or so that it took to perform the piece. He himself had been deeply moved by the experience.[2]

This statement helps us understand Messiaen's work as a triumph of humanity, however brief, over the inhumane conditions suffered by the prisoners of war. It also exemplifies the endurance of music in memory, in this case, its ability to bring back the time, place, and emotional impact of the original hearing. Were it not for this incredible moment, Lyczewski would most likely have forgotten January 15, 1941, as simply one in a long sequence of days filled with painful labor. Instead, his experience of Messiaen's music provoked a startling recall, a ray of hope that he remembered clearly more than forty years later.

The *Quartet for the End of Time* was also an expression of the composer's reli-gious faith. A devout Catholic, Messiaen derived the title of his quartet, and its inspiration, from a passage in the biblical Book of Revelation. Messiaen inscribed the music manuscript with a dedication "in homage to the Angel of the

Apocalypse, who raises a hand toward Heaven saying: 'There shall be time no longer.'" In the preface to the published score of the work, Messiaen included selections from this chapter:

> And I saw another mighty angel come down from heaven, clothed with a cloud; and a rainbow was upon his head, and his face was as it were the sun, and his feet as pillars of fire: . . . and he set his right foot upon the sea, and his left foot on the earth, . . . and the angel which I saw stand upon the sea and upon the earth lifted up his hand to heaven, and swore by him that liveth for ever and ever, . . . that there should be time no longer: but in the days of the voice of the seventh angel, when he shall begin to sound, the mystery of God should be finished.[3]

Thus, we could interpret the title of the *Quartet* in several ways. The most literal reference is to this apocalyptic vision, the moment when, according to Christian belief, the Savior returns to Earth and the world ends. The title also suggests the end of the composer's time of imprisonment, although Messiaen later denied that this word play was intended. In fact, a much more musical meaning was intended: the concept of time in (Western) musical terms is expressed by meter. The apocalyptic end of time, then, would be expressed musically by the breakdown—or actually the end—of meter. But music, being the arrangement of sounds in time, cannot exist without time, so we have a contradiction, a paradox. In any case, the absence of a regular meter in the *Quartet* greatly influences the sound of the composition.

The *Quartet* consists of eight movements, of which we will listen to the second. Titled *Vocalise for the Angel who Announces the End of Time*, it is one of the four movements that employs all four instruments simultaneously. It is divided into three sections, the first a relatively short introduction closely related to the third, a short conclusion. The second section, which is the bulk of the piece, sets the "timeless" mood. In the composer's words,

> The first and third sections (very short) evoke the power of the mighty Angel, crowned with a rainbow and clothed by a cloud, who sets one foot upon the sea and one foot upon the earth. In the middle section—these are the impalpable harmonies of heaven. On the piano, gentle cascades of blue-orange chords garland with their distant carillon the quasi-plainsong chanting of the violin and cello.[4]

The introductory passage consists of heavy, crashing chords on the piano, marked *modéré* ("moderate"), alternating with lighter passages, marked *presque vif* ("almost fast"), for violin and cello, which always play the same music but two octaves apart, and clarinet.

In the middle section, the piano produces a steady stream of chords that are evenly spaced but grouped into phrases of irregular lengths: many of the groups contain eight chords, some contain three, four, five, or another number, so that no regular pattern can be discerned. Meanwhile, the cello and violin play a melody in the upper parts of their ranges. This melody, which Messiaen compared to plain-chant, is the "vocalise" of the title—a song without words, normally for a singer to perform on a meaningless syllable like "la"—which may represent the voice of the angel. The stringed instruments are playing exactly the same melody but two octaves apart. We hear pitches of varying durations, out of sync with the chords in the piano part. Changes in the intensity, or, for that matter, any other aspect of the sound are minimal, resulting in a piece that conveys a truly static and timeless sensation.

In the concluding section, the instruments resume alternating quick and slow-er passages as in the first section. The musical ideas are the same as those in the first section but inverted; for example, in place of an ascending scale in the first section we now hear a descending one. In this way, the palindromic effect is achieved and the piece ends exactly where it began. The movement has formed a circle, and the "end of time" has been achieved.

LISTEN and notice that no regular meter with alternating strong and weak beats can be heard. The composer compared the melody to Gregorian chant, which is also performed without regular meter. In a real sense, the composition evokes a timelessness suggested by the composer's belief in the apocalypse. The rhythmic setting directly expresses the significance of the work.

CHAPTER

TEN TEN TEN TEN TEN TEN TEN TEN TEN TEN TEN TEN TEN TEN TEN TEN TEN TEN TEN

Music in the Real World

Over the past century and especially the past decade, new technologies and other factors have changed how we hear and perform music and how we understand its place in the world. Music can now be distributed quickly and easily to millions of people via recordings that can be played back by anyone at any time and can even be copied or downloaded on a computer at the click of a mouse. A performer may command an audience of a dozen in a small coffeehouse, reach fifty thousand people at a stadium concert, or touch millions of listeners during a live event that is transmitted to a global audience via radio, television, and the Internet. Western classical music has taken part in a full range of cultural exchanges that have resulted from our greatly increased ability to communicate. The demands of the new global music market have pushed Western classical music well beyond its former geographical and stylistic boundaries.

Duke Ellington's *Ko-Ko* and Leonard Bernstein's *West Side Story* both date from the mid-twentieth century, both have roots in Western classical music, but both have also drawn on other traditions. We will consider three levels of musical inter-action and influence. The *subcultural* influences of Duke Ellington's *Ko-Ko* are especially clear: a work for a classic, big-band jazz orchestra, *Ko-Ko* shows its roots in blues and has become a true standard among jazz performers. *Ko-Ko* reflects the local and personal musical worlds in which Ellington lived and composed. Leonard Bernstein, a Bostonian of Russian Jewish descent, grew up listening to the English operettas of Gilbert and Sullivan, received a thoroughly classical training as an orchestral conductor, and finally combined these influences with

Latin American dance rhythms, jazz harmonies, popular tunes, and modern dance to create *West Side Story* for Broadway. The musical truly brings together a wide variety of styles and cultural references on an *intercultural* level. Finally, commercialization and globalization have made both of these works available and influential around the world. The musics of Ellington and Bernstein, then, are well known on a *supercultural* level.

CASE STUDY:

Ko-Ko

The great international renown of Duke (Edward Kennedy) Ellington (1899–1974) was obvious at a New York City memorial service in May 1974 in the presence of ten thousand people. Another sixty-five thousand filed past his bier in the days before the service. The *New York Times* called Ellington "America's foremost composer" in its front-page obituary, and President Richard Nixon assured the world that the "memory of America's greatest composer" would live on for generations. Ellington was a driving force behind the development and popularization of jazz through much of the twentieth century.

The origins of jazz and other African American musical idioms are a matter of debate. The generations of slaves forcibly brought to America from Africa carried with them a rich heritage of language, music, and culture from their native lands. But this extraordinary diversity among early African Americans was largely lost through the brutality inflicted on them: families and communities were separated from their homes and each other by the slave trade itself and by slave owners, many of whom suppressed what musical traditions remained. Studies of African American music are just beginning to unravel the processes of changes and cultural contacts that transformed African singing styles, instrumental performance (including drumming), and storytelling techniques into work songs, early spirituals, and later gospel, ragtime, jazz, and rock. These processes are especially hard to reconstruct because little concerning early African American music was ever written down. Ironically, the influence of the European musical tradition on African American musics can be traced more easily because of its connection to the dominant culture.

A turning point in the career of the young pianist Duke Ellington came when he was hired in 1927 to perform at the elite Cotton Club in Harlem, a section of Manhattan populated mostly by African Americans. Although the white audiences were there to hear "exotic" music from the club's exclusively black performers, Ellington managed to produce innovative music and develop a unique big-band jazz style despite the club's restrictions. As Ellington's band became famous in the 1930s, his compositional style moved from a largely improvised genre to works based on a written score. The *score* (musical notation) for *Ko-Ko* does not follow the usual classical convention of listing the instruments to be used in performing the piece. Instead, Ellington wrote in the names of the band members who were to play each part. This practice, standard in Ellington's scores, reflects the highly personal nature of his compositions. Each musician in his band had a unique performance style and specialized in producing certain special effects, and Ellington's music was designed to take advantage of each player's particular talent.

Ko-Ko was first recorded in the early 1940s during an intensely productive period in the recording studio for Ellington and his band. The group includes five saxophones (2 altos, 2 tenors, and a baritone), three trumpets, three trombones, guitar, bass, drums, and Ellington himself on piano. The work is an excellent example of what was called a "jungle style," perfected during the Cotton Club years with an emphasis on special effects in the trumpet and trombone sections. These included the "wah-wah" and "yah-yah" sounds produced by playing these instruments with a *plunger mute,* a piece of rubber from a toilet-plunger that is used to cover or partially cover the bell (the wide opening at the end) of a brass instrument. These sounds can be said to resemble human voices.

The piece is based on a twelve-bar blues progression, a basic harmonic pattern described in chapter 8. After a short introduction, in *Ko-Ko* this pattern repeats over and over until we have heard it eight times, or through eight *choruses,* as these sections are called in jazz. A distinctive rhythmic motive also appears throughout the piece. This short-short-short-long idea can be heard at the very beginning of the recording in the *tom-tom* (a type of drum); it is repeated by the baritone saxophone several times during the introduction. The motive, as you may have noticed, is rhythmically identical to the first notes of both *When the Saints Go Marching In* and Beethoven's Fifth Symphony! We will probably never know whether Ellington copied the rhythm by accident or on purpose.

Ko-Ko is widely considered to be among Ellington's finest works, because it effectively manipulates a few simple musical ideas without becoming repetitive or boring. Songs based on a twelve-bar blues form can be predictable, and the deceptive simplicity of the short-short-short-long motive might have been a problem for a less talented composer. But Ellington subtly tinkers with the syncopated responses, enlivens the orchestration, and effectively balances a variety of musical styles, weaving a complex fabric from a minimum of musical material and keeping the piece interesting throughout.

It is clear that Ellington used a variety of musical languages in this work. Ellington took the phrase "beyond category" to be a great compliment. He avoided using "jazz" as a category to describe his music, preferring to call his work "Negro folk music." His thousand-plus compositions do not neatly fit such limited categories as "jazz standards" or "dance tunes." He wrote works for symphony orchestras and for piano solo; he composed movie soundtracks, sacred cantatas, and incidental music for plays by Shakespeare and T. S. Eliot; he even reinterpreted works by classical composers Peter Tchaikovsky and Edvard Grieg. In many ways, then Ellington epitomized the twentieth-century American composer interacting with the real world.

LISTEN FOR the call-and-response technique heard throughout *Ko-Ko* as you follow the prominent features of the piece:

> Introduction—baritone saxophone plays the main motive on a single low note, with chordal commentary from the trombones.
> Chorus 1—valve trombone calls the main motive, with homophonic sax quintet responding.
> Chorus 2—one muted trombone calls "ya-ya" with saxophone accompaniment, while trumpets and other trombones respond with syncopated chords.
> Chorus 3—same instrumentation as chorus 2, with growing intensity and different sound quality because of changed mute position.
> Chorus 4—saxophones call, trumpets respond, then Ellington piano solo cuts through with unusual harmonies, percussive chords, and quick scale passages.
> Chorus 5—trumpets call in unison, saxophones and trombones respond.
> Chorus 6—saxophone call and brass response interrupted by a sudden break and a short bass solo; heard three times.
> Chorus 7—slightly modified call in the brass, three saxophones give a lively response.
> Chorus 8—as in introduction, baritone sax plays one-vote version of motive, trombones respond, other instruments enter and the full band ends the piece.

CASE STUDY:

Mambo and *Tonight* from *West Side Story*

Leonard Bernstein (1918–1990), like Ellington, created a uniquely American music by fusing classical techniques with ideas from other soundscapes. By the early 1950s, Bernstein had earned an international reputation as an outstanding conductor with such orchestras as the Israel Philharmonic, the Boston Symphony, and the New York Philharmonic, and had conducted opera at La Scala in Milan. He also gained renown as a composer, as some twenty of his compositions were performed between 1942 and 1957, all but one of them dramatic or programmatic.

West Side Story was Bernstein's third Broadway musical. The story of its creation exemplifies the process by which compositions can be completely changed because of seemingly insignificant real-world events. Some time between 1949 and 1952, the choreographer Jerome Robbins approached Bernstein about collaborating on a modern musical adaptation of Shakespeare's *Romeo and Juliet*. In the musical, religious tension in urban America was to be depicted through two feuding families, Catholic "Capulets" and Jewish "Montagues." The action was to be set in the tenements of the Upper East Side of Manhattan, and the musical was tentatively titled *East Side Story*. Bernstein and Robbins began meeting with playwright Arthur Laurents, but the play was not taking shape as they had hoped and so, a few months later, the project was shelved.

While visiting California a few years later, Bernstein read a newspaper article about gang warfare between white Los Angelenos and Mexican immigrants. He saw an opportunity to incorporate Latin-American dance rhythms into the piece and, excited by the new possibilities, resumed work on *East Side Story,* this time with Steven Sondheim as the lyricist for Laurents's book.

At the time, tenements on the East Side were being torn down to make room for more upscale housing projects. The team of Robbins, Bernstein, Laurents, and Sondheim decided to change the plot to focus on the rapidly growing Puerto Rican community that was moving into the West Side, and thus *West Side Story* was born. Bernstein's familiarity with the sounds and rhythms of New York City came through clearly. Like Reich's *City Life, West Side Story* is a truly urban music reflecting the vitality of a particular locale. It opened on Broadway on September 26, 1957, to rave reviews, and the initial run totaled 732 performances.

The plot clearly parallels that of *Romeo and Juliet*. A Puerto Rican gang, the Sharks, is feuding with a white gang, the Jets. Tony, a Jet, falls in love with Maria, whose brother is the leader of the Sharks. The first excerpt on our recording is the *Mambo,* a dance of Cuban origin that rose to international popularity in the 1940s. Choreographer Robbins played on the relationship between love and war as the Jets and the Sharks danced and squared off against each other on stage.

The dance begins with a fanfare-like percussion solo. The strong, danceable meter overrides the complex Latin syncopations that we hear throughout the piece. Percussion instruments, even including hand-clapping, continually emphasize this syncopation. Also, bold instrumentation, as in Ellington's *Ko-Ko,* pits winds and brass against each other. When one group is playing the melody, the other is usually constructing an elaborate commentary on it. Onstage, the gangs' shouts of "Mam-bo!" make for a surprising change in texture; later in the dance, the outburst "Go, Mam-bo!" adds complexity as a triple meter is layered on top of the established duple meter. The piece ends with a drop in intensity as the gangs depart, leaving Tony and Maria alone.

The second excerpt, *Tonight,* prefaces the "Rumble," the big fight and the climax of Act I. The music portrays the growing tension between the gangs through the insistent, repetitive bass line (played by trombones and bassoons) and through the mens' rough-edged vocal style. The first half of the work consists of five verses and one refrain, sung in an antiphonal style; all verses except the third are set to the same music. Throughout the verses, the meter frequently shifts between groups of six, four, and three beats, helping to convey the instability of the dramatic situation.

The second half of the work is a quintet for the Jets, the Sharks, Anita, Tony, and Maria. For this piece, Bernstein was certainly influenced by earlier operatic ensemble scenes. While Maria and Tony sing the melody of the refrain, the other three parts (Riff/Jets, Anita/women, and Sharks) create layer upon layer of sound.

Verse 1

Jets:	The Jets are gonna have their day Tonight.
Sharks:	The Sharks are gonna have their way Tonight.
Jets:	The Puerto Ricans grumble: "Fair fight."
	But if they start a rumble,
	We'll rumble 'em right.

Verse 2

Sharks:	We're gonna hand 'em a surprise Tonight.
Jets:	We're gonna cut 'em down to size Tonight.
Sharks:	We said, "O.K., no rumpus, no tricks."
	But just in case they jump us,
	We're ready to mix—Tonight!

Verse 3—variation

Ensemble:	We're gonna rock it tonight,
	We're gonna jazz it up and have us a ball!
	They're gonna get it tonight;
	The more they turn it on, the harder they'll fall!
Jets:	Well, they began it!
Sharks:	Well, they began it!
Ensemble:	And we're the ones to stop 'em once and for all,
	Tonight!

Verse 4

Anita:

> Anita's gonna get her kicks Tonight.
> We'll have our private little mix Tonight.
> He'll walk in hot and tired, So what?
> Don't matter if he's tired,
> As long as he's hot—Tonight!

Refrain

Tony:

> (a) Tonight, tonight
>   Won't be just any night,
>   Tonight there will be no morning star.
> (a) Tonight, tonight,
>   I'll see my love tonight
>   And for us, stars will stop where they are.
> (b) Today the minutes seem like hours,
>   The hours go so slowly,
>   And still the sky is light.
> (a) Oh moon, grow bright,
>   And make this endless day endless night!

Verse 5

Jets:

> We're counting on you to be there Tonight
> When Diesel wins it fair and square Tonight.
> That Puerto Rican punk'll
> Go down
> And when he's hollered "Uncle"
> We'll tear up the town!

Quintet:

Maria

> *Refrain:*
> Tonight, tonight
> Won't be just any night,
> Tonight there will be no morning star.
> Tonight, tonight
> I'll see my love tonight
> And for us, stars will stop where they are.

(With Tony)

> Today the minutes seem like hours,
> The hours go so slowly,
> And still the sky is light.

Oh moon, grow bright,
And make this endless day endless night!
Tonight!

Simultaneously:

Riff:	So I can count on you, boy?	Sharks:	Tonight! They began it,
Tony:	All right.	Women:	Anita's gonna have her day,
Riff:	We're gonna have us a ball.	Men:	They began it,
Tony:	All right.		And we're the ones
Riff:	(Spoken) Womb to tomb!		To stop 'em once and for all!
Tony:	(Spoken) Sperm to worm!	Women:	Bernardo's gonna have his way
Riff:	I'll see you there about eight.		Tonight, tonight.
Tony:	Tonight.	Men:	The (Jets/Sharks) are gonna
Sharks:	We're gonna rock it tonight!		have their way,
Women:	Tonight,		The (Jets/Sharks) are gonna
Sharks:	We're gonna jazz it tonight!		have their day,
Women:	Tonight, Late tonight,	Women:	Tonight, this very night,
Sharks:	They're gonna get it tonight,		We're gonna rock it tonight!
Women:	We're gonna mix it tonight.	Men:	Tonight!

Cuban dance rhythms, jazz harmonies, New York sensibilities, classical Broadway choreography, and formal operatic conventions all come together in *West Side Story*. The musical was a great success on Broadway, and the film version won the Oscar for Best Picture of 1961 as well as nine other Academy Awards. The global success of the movie underscores the real-world impact that the communication technology of its day had on musical awareness around the world.

LISTEN TO the way Maria and Tony react only to each other—both musically and dramatically—during the quintet, while the other voices ignore them. In a sense, several monologues are going on simultaneously, and the overall effect underlines the characters' emotional responses to the situation.

ADDITIONAL IMPORTANT TERMS

bell (trumpet or trombone)   lyricist

big band   plunger mute

chorus (jazz)   score

jungle style   tom-tom

Notes

CHAPTER THREE

[1]Tibbetts, 1993, 40.
[2]Dvorak in Tibbets 362–63.
[3]Reprinted in Nomura, 1956, 466.

CHAPTER FOUR

[1]Copland and Perlis, 1984, 245.
[2]Copland and Perlis, 1984, 280.
[3]Copland, "Notes on a Cowboy Ballet," Copland Collection at the Library of Congress. Reprinted in Pollack, 1999, 320.

CHAPTER SIX

[6]Quoted in Landon, 1984, 89–90, and Hogwood, 1984, 71–72.

CHAPTER EIGHT

[1]Excerpt from *Písen svobody* (The Song of Freedom), text by Jan Kollár, quoted in Large, 1970, 45.
[2]Translated and printed in Large, 1970, 273.
[3]Much of this discussion of *Carmen* and the *Habañera* are based on McClary 1992, 33–57 passim.

CHAPTER NINE

[1]Gutman, 1988, 124–25.
[2]Quoted in Pople 1998, 16.
[3]Revelation 10: 1–7.
[4]Messiaen, preface to the miniature score of the *Quartet* (Paris: Durand, 1942): 1. Reprinted in Pople, 1998, 28.

Sources and
Works Cited

GENERAL WORKS

The New Grove Dictionary of Music and Musicians. 2nd ed. London: Macmillan, 2001.
  (Abbreviated *TNG* below.)
Randel, Don Michael. *The Harvard Concise Dictionary of Music and Musicians*.
  Cambridge: Harvard University Press, 1999.
Forney, Kristine, ed. *The Norton Scores*. 8th ed. New York: W. W. Norton, 1999.
Grout, Donald Jay, and Claude V. Palisca. *A History of Western Music*. 6th ed. New York:
  W. W. Norton, 2001.
Machlis, Joseph, and Kristine Forney. *The Enjoyment of Music*. 8th ed. Standard. New
  York: W. W. Norton, 1999.

CHAPTER 1

Carpenter, Humphrey. *Benjamin Britten: A Biography*. London: Faber and Faber, 1992.
Raynor, Henry. *Music and Society since 1815*. London: Barrie & Jenkins, 1976.

Arnold, Denis. *Monteverdi Madrigals*. BBC Music Guides. London: British Broadcasting
  Corporation, 1967.
———. *Monteverdi*. 3rd ed., rev. Tim Carter. The Master Musicians. London: J. M. Dent,
  1990.
Arnold, Denis, and Elsie M. Arnold. "Monteverdi, Claudio." In *TNG*.
Arnold, Denis, and Nigel Fortune, eds. *The Monteverdi Companion*. London: Faber and
  Faber, 1968.

Carter, Tim. *Music in Late Renaissance and Early Baroque Italy.* London: B. T. Batsford, 1992.

Fisher, Kurt von; James Haar; and Anthony Newcomb. "Madrigal," I and II. In *TNG.*

Horton, John. *Monteverdi.* Novello Short Biographies. Borough Green, Eng.: Novello, 1975.

CHAPTER 2

Banks, Paul, and Donald Mitchell. "Mahler, Gustav." In *TNG.*

Raynor, Henry. *Mahler.* London: Macmillan, 1975.

Seckerson, Edward. *Mahler: His Life and Times.* New York: Hippocrene Books, 1982.

Everett, Paul. *Vivaldi: "The Four Seasons" and Other Concertos, Op. 8.* Cambridge Music Handbooks. Cambridge: Cambridge University Press, 1996.

Heller, Karl. *Antonio Vivaldi: The Red Priest of Venice.* Trans. David Marinelli. Portland, Ore.: Amadeus Press, 1997.

CHAPTER 3

Beckerman, Michael, ed. *Dvořák and His World.* Princeton: Princeton University Press, 1993.

Beveridge, David R., ed. *Rethinking Dvořák: Views from Five Countries.* Oxford: Clarendon Press, 1996.

Dvorakin Tibbets 362_63

Ivanov, Miroslav. *In Dvořák's Footsteps: Musical Journeys in the New World.* Trans. Stania Slahor, ed. Leon Karel. Kirksville, Mo.: Thomas Jefferson University Press, 1995.

Tibbetts, John C., ed. *Dvořák in America, 1892–1895.* Portland, Ore.: Amadeus Press, 1993.

Coaldrake, A. Kimi. "Building a New Musical Tradition: The Sōgakudō and the Introduction of Western Music in Japan." *Musicology Australia* 13 (1990): 35–41.

Eppstein, Ury. *The Beginnings of Western Music in Meiji Era Japan.* Lewiston, N.Y.: E. Mellen Press, 1994.

Hattori, Koh-Ichi. *36,000 Days of Japanese Music.* Southfield, Mich.: Pacific Vision Books, 1996.

Hedley, Arthur, and Maurice J. E. Brown. "Chopin, Fryderyk Franciszek." In *TNG.*

Nomura, Koichi. "Occidental Music." In *Japanese Culture in the Meiji Era.* Vol. 3: *Music and Drama,* ed. Komiya Toyotaka. Trans. Edward G. Seidensticker and Donald Keene. Tokyo: Obunsha, 1956.

Takatoshi, Yoshida. "How Western Music Came to Japan." *Tempo* 40 (Summer 1956): 16–17.

CHAPTER 4

Beecher, Donald. "Edition Notes." In *The Cries of London,* by Orlando Gibbons. Hannacroix, N.Y.: Loux Music Company; Ottawa, Ont.: Dove House Editions, 1997.

Reich, Steve. *Writings about Music*. Halifax: Press of Nova Scotia College of Art and Design, 1994.

———. Liner notes for *City Life*. CD. Nonesuch 79430-2. 1996.

Schwarz, K. Robert. *Minimalists*. London: Phaidon Press, 1996.

Copland, Aaron, and Vivian Perlis. *Copland: 1900 through 1942*. New York: St. Martin's Press/Marek, 1984.

Pollack, Howard. *Aaron Copland: The Life and Work of an Uncommon Man*. New York: Henry Holt, 1999.

Worcester, Donald Emmet. *The Chisholm Trail: High Road of the Cattle Kingdom*. Lincoln: University of Nebraska Press, 1980.

CHAPTER 5

Hoppin, Richard H. *Medieval Music*. New York: W. W. Norton, 1978.

Coates, Henry. *Palestrina*. London: J. M. Dent, 1938.

Lang, Paul Henry. "Palestrina across the Centuries." In *Festschrift Karl Gustav Fellerer zum sechzigsten Geburtstag am 7. Juli 1962,* ed. Heinrich Hüschen. Regensburg: G. Bosse, 1962. Pp. 294–302.

Lockwood, Lewis, and Jessie Ann Owens. "Palestrina, Giovanni Pierluigi da." In *TNG*.

Palestrina, Giovanni Pierluigi da. *Pope Marcellus Mass: An Authoritative Score*. Lewis Lockwood, ed. New York: W. W. Norton, 1975.

CHAPTER 6

Cessac, Catherine. *Elisabeth Jacquet de la Guerre: Une Femme Compositeur sous le règne de Louis XIV.* Arles: Actes Sud, 1995.

Harris-Warrick, Rebecca, and Carol G. Marsh. *Musical Theatre at the Court of Louis XIV: Le mariage de la Gros Cathos*. Cambridge: Cambridge University Press, 1994.

Jezic, Diane Peacock. *Women Composers: The Lost Tradition Found*. 2nd ed., ed. Elizabeth Wood. New York: The Feminist Press at The City University of New York, 1994.

Little, Meredith Ellis. "Gigue." In *TNG*.

Dean, Winton. *The New Grove Handel*. New York: W. W. Norton, 1983.

Dean-Smith, Margaret. "Hornpipe." In *TNG*.

Hogwood, Christopher. *Handel*. London: Thames and Hudson, 1984.

Landon, H. C. Robbins. *Handel and His World*. London: Weidenfeld and Nicolson, 1984.

CHAPTER 7

Bach, Johann Sebastian. *Ein feste Burg ist unser Gott: Cantata 80*, ed. Arnold Schering. London: E. Eulenburg, 1926.

Chafe, Eric. *Analyzing Bach Cantatas*. New York: Oxford University Press, 2000.

Marshall, Robert L. *Luther, Bach, and the Early Reformation Chorale*. Atlanta: Pitts Theology Library, 1995.

Robertson, Alec. *The Church Cantatas of J. S. Bach*. London: Cassell, 1972.

Wolff, Christoph. *Johann Sebastian Bach: The Learned Musician*. New York: W. W. Norton, 2000.

Arnold, Denis, and Nigel Fortune, eds. *The Beethoven Reader*. New York: W. W. Norton, 1971.

Comini, Alessandra. *The Changing Image of Beethoven*: A Study in Mythmaking. New York: Rizzoli, 1987.

James, Burnett. *Beethoven and Human Destiny*. New York: Roy Publishers, 1961.

Chapter 8

Clapham, John. *Smetana*. London: J. M. Dent, 1972.

Large, Brian. *Smetana*. London: Duckworth, 1970.

Malý, Miloslav. *Bedřich Smetana*. Prague: Orbis, 1956.

Dean, Winton. "Bizet, Georges." In *TNG*.

McClary, Susan. *Georges Bizet, Carmen*. Cambridge: Cambridge University Press, 1992.

Chapter 9

Nichols, Roger. *Messiaen*. Oxford Studies of Composers. Oxford: Oxford University Press, 1986.

Pople, Anthony. *Messiaen: Quatuor pour la fin du temps*. Cambridge Music Handbooks. Cambridge: Cambridge University Press, 1998.

Brown, Royal S. *Overtones and Undertones: Reading Film Music*. Berkeley: University of California Press, 1994.

Egorova, Tatiana K. *Soviet Film Music: An Historical Survey*. Trans. Tatiana A. Ganf and Natalia A. Egunova. Amsterdam: Harwood Academic Publishers, 1997.

Gutman, David. *Prokofiev*. London: Alderman Press, 1988.

Jaffé, Daniel. *Sergey Prokofiev*. London: Phaidon Press, 1998.

Shmidt, S. O. "Alexander Nevsky." In *Great Soviet Encyclopedia*, ed. A. M. Prokhorov. 3rd ed. New York: Macmillan, 1970.

Chapter 10

Collier, James Lincoln. *Duke Ellington*. Oxford: Oxford University Press, 1987.

Rattenbury, Ken. *Duke Ellington: Jazz Composer*. New Haven: Yale University Press, 1990.

Steed, Janna Tull. *Duke Ellington: A Spiritual Biography*. New York: Crossroad, 1999.

Bernstein, Shirley. *Making Music: Leonard Bernstein*. Chicago: Encyclopedia Britannica Press, 1963.

Meyers, Paul. *Leonard Bernstein*. London: Phaidon Press, 1998.